SÖREN
KIERKEGAARD

Makers of the Modern Theological Mind
Bob E. Patterson, Editor

KARL BARTH by *David L. Mueller*
DIETRICH BONHOEFFER by *Dallas M. Roark*
RUDOLF BULTMANN by *Morris Ashcraft*
CHARLES HARTSHORNE by *Alan Gragg*
WOLFHART PANNENBERG by *Don Olive*
TEILHARD DE CHARDIN by *Doran McCarty*
EMIL BRUNNER by *J. Edward Humphrey*
MARTIN BUBER by *Stephen M. Panko*
SÖREN KIERKEGAARD by *Elmer H. Duncan*
REINHOLD NIEBUHR by *Bob E. Patterson*

Makers of the Modern Theological Mind

Bob E. Patterson, Editor

SÖREN KIERKEGAARD

by Elmer H. Duncan

With an Additional Chapter by
Danny Floyd Walker

Word Books, Publisher, Waco, Texas

SÖREN KIERKEGAARD

ISBN 0–87680–463–6
Library of Congress catalog card number: 76–2862
Printed in the United States of America

*For Rosemary and Beverly
—and Alyssa—
and Jason and Marc—and the
girls of Sigma Tau Lambda*

When I once quoted to him a remark of Kierkegaard to this effect: "How can it be that Christ does not exist, since I know that He has saved me?", Wittgenstein exclaimed: "You see! It isn't a question of *proving* anything!"

Norman Malcolm
in his
Ludwig Wittgenstein: A Memoir

Contents

Editor's Preface

Who are the thinkers that have shaped Christian theology in our time? This series tries to answer that question by providing a reliable guide to the ideas of the men who have significantly charted the theological seas of our century. In the current revival of theology, these books will give a new generation the opportunity to be exposed to significant minds. They are not meant, however, to be a substitute for a careful study of the original works of these makers of the modern theological mind.

This series is not for the lazy. Each major theologian is examined carefully and critically—his life, his theological method, his most germinal ideas, his weaknesses as a thinker, his place in the theological spectrum, and his chief contribution to the climate of theology today. The books are written with the assumption that laymen will read them and enter into the theological dialogue that is so necessary to the church as a whole. At the same time they are carefully enough designed to give assurance to a Ph.D. student in theology preparing for his preliminary exams.

Each author in the series is a professional scholar and theologian in his own right. All are specialists on, and in some cases have studied with, the theologians about whom they write. Welcome to the series.

BOB E. PATTERSON, Editor
Baylor University

Preface

When Bob Patterson asked me to do a book on Kierkegaard, I was delighted. Since I had written my doctoral dissertation on Kierkegaard under the direction of two of America's finest philosophers, Professors Van Meter Ames and Joseph Margolis, I could foresee no problems in simply presenting the dissertation as a book.

But there *were* difficulties. For one thing, the dissertation was more than ten years old, and much has happened in those ten years. As the reader will see in the chapters that follow, much of what I wrote in my 1962 dissertation, and in published articles, still seems to me to be true, but strangely beside the point. So I had to take a fresh look from an entirely different perspective. Further, Kierkegaard was both a philosopher *and* a theologian; I am only a philosopher. Though I *am* a churchman, I am not a trained theologian. Kierkegaard can, I am convinced, best be understood as a philosopher who has had a terrific impact on contemporary theology. From the first I felt that I could set forth and evaluate his philosophical position in a clear way, but I came to feel that I could not fully appreciate his impact on current theology. So I persuaded Professor Patterson to permit me to use a co-author. I asked Dan Walker to do a chapter on Kierkegaard's influence on contemporary theology. This chapter makes clear the sense in which Kierkegaard deserves to be numbered among the "Makers of the Modern Theological Mind."

Dan seems ideally suited for the task. He has a B.D. from Southwestern Seminary and is now a doctoral candidate in Religion at Baylor University. He has also taken a number of courses in philosophy, including a graduate seminar in Existentialism which I taught some years ago. While working on his doctorate here, Dan teaches philosophy at McLennan Community College.

A preface is perhaps the place for an author to express appreciation to those who have helped him. Unfortunately, I owe so much to so many people that I cannot do this in detail in the present book. I must, however, thank my chairman at Baylor, Prof. William J. Kilgore, who has always supported my work. Thanks are also due to Mr. and Mrs. J. Newton Rayzor, whose financial support of the Philosophy Department made possible the preparation of this manuscript. Of course, the manuscript would not have been as well prepared as it is had I not been fortunate enough to have the services of two of the world's finest secretaries, Beth Ingalls and Marilyn Ender.

I'm sure that my co-author, Dan Walker, would agree that our greatest debt is to our wives, Rosemary and Beverly. However unorthodox this may be, I also wish to express appreciation to some of the other women in my life. First, I want to thank my mother, who gave me religious values, even though she didn't make me a theologian. Then I must thank Miss

Norene Newberry, who (back in the second grade!) first taught me the value of academic achievement and then spent several summers in a little Baptist church in South Shore, Kentucky, teaching me that the Bible deserved serious study, too. I was able to make it through college and graduate school primarily because—whatever faults I had—I could *read;* I owe this to Miss Newberry and to my high school English teacher, Mrs. Lena Nevison. Finally, if I ever lose sight of what Christianity really is, I can regain my vision by attending the weekly meetings of Sigma Tau Lambda, the social and service club of the School of Nursing here at Baylor, which my wife and I have had the high honor of sponsoring these past several years. These are the women in my life; I know that Kierkegaard would have loved them all . . . and so do I.

E. H. D.

I. Life

THE SINS OF THE FATHER

Sören Kierkegaard's story begins with his father, and not simply in the trivial sense that we all have fathers, who are likely to influence our lives. This was a case of a father having a decisive hand in shaping the life of his son.

As a boy, Michael Pedersen Kierkegaard was a shepherd in the parish of Saeding in Jutland. The town (if it could be called a town) had its Danish Lutheran Church, but it was too poor to have a regular pastor. So the little parsonage was rented and the family which occupied it took the churchyard (Kirkegaard) in which it stood as their family name. The letter *e* was later added to the name for social reasons.

The life of a shepherd on the frozen heaths of Jutland must have been cold and hard. One night, young Michael gave vent to his anger and frustration by cursing God. This event cannot be overemphasized, for Michael Pedersen Kierkegaard was convinced that he had committed the unpardonable sin.

A hard life often produces a hard and unyielding religion;
the elder Kierkegaard thought of God as "by no means clear-
ing the guilty, visiting the iniquity of the fathers upon the
children unto the third and fourth generation" (Num. 14:18).
Kierkegaard's father had a deep sense of guilt and sorrow,
which never left him, though he lived to be eighty-two. This
he passed on to his sons.

But strangely, after he had cursed God, things took a turn
for the better for young Michael Kierkegaard. His family decided that they could no longer afford even to feed and clothe
the boy, so he was sent to live with his uncle in Copenhagen.
The uncle was in the clothing business—a hosier, actually.
Michael did amazingly well in his new role, prospering beyond his wildest dreams. The business was broadened from
hosiery to clothing in general—all types—and greatly expanded. When the uncle died, the business passed on to young
Michael, who continued to expand it, adding a chain of gro-
cery stores. He got married, bought a fine large house, and
amassed such a fortune that he was able to retire at the age
of forty.

This incredible prosperity did not continue uninterrupted,
however. The wife died, childless, after less than two years
of marriage. Before the end of another year, Michael had re-
married. The plain truth, crudely put, is that he seduced one
of his servants, and had to marry her. She bore him a daughter in just over four months of marriage. The date was Sep-
tember 7, 1797. During the next few years, Ane Sörensdatter
(Lund) Kierkegaard bore her husband seven children in all,
three daughters and four sons. The last son, born May 5, 1813,
was Sören Aabye Kierkegaard.

Marriages of this type are rarely happy, and this one was
not. Apparently Kierkegaard's father continued to think of his

wife as a servant. (It may be worth noting that in all his voluminous writings, Kierkegaard had little or nothing to say about his mother.) For all that, things seemed to go well with the Kierkegaards for many years. They were respected and wealthy and must have been the envy of much of Copenhagen.

Sören Kierkegaard was, then, one of seven children, but before he had completed his twenty-first year, no less than five of the children, and their mother, were dead. The causes of their deaths ranged from playground accidents to childbirth but one by one they died. None of them lived beyond the age of thirty-three. Only Sören and his older brother Peter (eight years his senior) were left with their aging father.

It is not clear whether the old man confessed to them, or they only guessed the truth, but somehow the sons came to know the sins of their father. Not surprisingly, they too believed that they would die young.

For much of his life, Sören Kierkegaard kept journals. They were not diaries; the entries were not often dated, and they were not kept regularly. In these *Journals* Kierkegaard often expressed shock at being still alive. S.K. (if I may abbreviate, and this is the standard abbreviation) was never a well man. He was short of stature and had an abnormal curvature of the spine. Beyond this, but perhaps connected with it, S.K. often spoke of the "thorn in the flesh" which troubled him throughout his life. We do not know precisely what his illness was. He was always frail, yet he worked very hard. He collapsed several times in public in the years just before his death, and asked to be swept under the furniture until he recovered. In the end, an old man at forty-two, he was carried, paralyzed, to the Frederiks Hospital, where he died November 11, 1855.

No attempt is being made here to write a biography of

Sören Kierkegaard. This has been done, and extremely well, by Walter Lowrie. Actually, Dr. Lowrie has done our work for us twice. He wrote a lengthy biography in 1938, incorporating a great deal of quoted material (which Lowrie translated himself) from Kierkegaard's writings. By 1942, Lowrie thought that enough of these writings were available in English that he could omit some of his quotations—and much detailed analysis, I might add—in his *Short Life of Sören Kierkegaard.* Now Ronald Grimsley has added his *Kierkegaard: A Biographical Introduction* (1973), so a lengthy biography is not needed. I shall, accordingly, restrict myself to a few aspects of Kierkegaard's life and personality which are indispensable for understanding his thought.

It was the wish of Kierkegaard's father that he be trained for the ministry. So he became, in 1830, a student at the University of Copenhagen, ostensibly with the purpose of becoming a minister. But though he studied theology, he seems to have enjoyed philosophy more. He also loved literature, the theater, and opera. S.K.'s personality was complex. Though melancholy, and burdened with his father's guilt, he was also a wit who loved the night life of his city. Though deeply religious—and he did finally pass his theological examination—he never felt called to preach. He never took a pastorate.

THE PLAYBOY AUTHOR OF *EDIFYING DISCOURSES*

But Kierkegaard *did* think of himself as called, that is, he considered himself a man with a God-given mission. His mission was to help people to become Christians, but he was to do this through his writing, not through preaching. He thought it important to emphasize the fact that he was not asking anyone to follow him, or his example. In his writing, therefore, he never posed as a minister writing sermons and teaching by example. Instead, he wrote what he called *Edifying Discourses*, and he insisted these were, in a sense, without authority. In his greatest works—which I take to be his *Either/Or, Fear and Trembling, The Philosophical Fragments*, and *Concluding Unscientific Postscript*—he hid his authorship behind pseudonyms. He did not, again, want to be in the position of teaching a *system* of thought, which he exemplified in his own life. He taught by the use of what he liked to call "indirect communication." He thought of Christianity not as a doctrine to be learned but a life to be lived, a way of life to be chosen. So he told stories, and through his pseudonyms set forth various life-styles, so that the reader would see that he had a choice to make.

Perhaps all of this would be clearer if it were contrasted with its opposite. Suppose for a moment that I were a learned professor of theology, and wanted you to become a Christian. To me this means accepting the Christian doctrine, so I run through various proofs that God exists, and that the Bible is his word. You, the reader, are expected to accept all of this on the basis of the rationale and intellectual rigor of my proofs *and* on the authority of my status as a scholar (with an impressive list of degrees) and as a churchman, witness to the truth, etc.

But, Kierkegaard thought, all of this is a mistake. Christianity is not a doctrine to be taught, but rather a life to be lived. "Proofs" then, are not only unconvincing: they are irrelevant, completely beside the point. Finally, how can any mortal man dare to set himself up as the model for living such a life? As usual, S.K. said it better than his interpreters, when he wrote in the preface to his *Philosophical Fragments*:

But if anyone were to be so polite as to assume that I have an opinion, and if he were to carry his gallantry to the extreme of adopting this opinion because he believed it to be mine, I should have to be sorry for his politeness, in that it was bestowed upon so unworthy an object, and for his opinion, if he has no other opinion than mine.[1]

Kierkegaard worked very hard at *not* being taken as a model for the Christian life. In addition to using pseudonyms, he went to great lengths to pretend to be a playboy, or man about town, or ne'er-do-well. In his short lifetime, he wrote a whole shelf of books, so he obviously spent long hours in work, study, and writing. To keep up his public image, however, he made it a practice to put in an appearance at every party, opera, and play. He would "make the rounds," so to speak, making sure that he was seen by everyone, and then return home to his work. At the conclusion of his *Postscript* he admitted authorship of the works cited above (plus others) but up to then, he must have been thought of as Copenhagen's biggest loafer—though the truth is he may have worked himself to death, and died of sheer exhaustion.

THE ENGAGEMENT

The vital statistics of a man's life must include his marriage. S.K. never had one. The great love of his life was Regina Olsen (her name was really Regine, only S.K. called her Regina). Apparently S.K. loved her very deeply; certainly his *Journals* indicate that he did. They became engaged to be married, but S.K. broke the engagement. Regina wept bitterly, said that she would surely die, and she and her father pleaded with S.K. to go on with the wedding. He remained firm in his refusal. A few years later, she married another

man, but S.K. never married. The *Journals* show that he
never forgot her, nor did he cease to love her.

It is a favorite game among Kierkegaard scholars to try to
discover why S.K. broke off the engagement. At the time of
the engagement he was twenty-four, Regina only fourteen
years of age. Perhaps he simply felt that the difference in age
and the contrast between her youthful spirit and his melancholy would make for an unhappy marriage—and remember
that he was convinced that he had not long to live. In the
Journals there is an account of a young man who became drunk
at a party and was then carried by his friends to a brothel,
where he had intercourse with a prostitute. Thereafter, he was
burdened with guilt, and with the fear that somewhere there
was a child of this illicit union that should have borne his
name. Some scholars assume that the story was autobiographical and that this was the reason S.K. could not marry Regina.
Perhaps—but the *Journals* were not entirely autobiographical,
and we need not assume that this story was true of S.K.
himself.

In his biography Grimsley discusses the intriguing suggestion that the story may have been true of S.K.'s father. This
would explain a great deal. Perhaps this sexual sin had led
to a dread disease which had caused the death of the other
children of the family. The young Sören could only wait, help-
lessly, to see its terrible effects begin to emerge in his own
life. As Grimsley explains:

> Needless to say, this supposition of a hereditary trait could have
> been without adequate foundation, for there is no surviving
> medical evidence to suggest that Kierkegaard or even his father
> suffered from any infection of this kind, but the mere belief in
> such a possibility would be enough to explain its enormous im-
> portance for both men. It would certainly account for Sören's

refusal to marry Regine. How could he confide to her a secret of
this kind, one that concerned not only himself but also his father
and the whole family? [2]

My own view is that S.K. simply became convinced that
marriage was not consistent with his divine mission. Kierkegaard often expressed admiration for Roman Catholic priests
who renounced marriage for the sake of their calling. He
probably would not have been sympathetic with the revolution
in this area that is rocking the Catholic Church today. And,
as we shall see below, he was critical of his own Danish Lutheran Church because its ministers, rather then renouncing
the pleasures of this world (a home, wife, respected public
position, ample means, etc.), had, he thought, perverted the
teachings of Christ by becoming state officials.

THE *ATTACK UPON CHRISTENDOM*

The *Journals* indicate that Kierkegaard was convinced,
for much of his life, that the state church, the Danish
Lutheran Church, was in a sorry condition. The leader of
this church was the Bishop Primate, the Most Reverend J. P.
Mynster. S.K. grew up hearing his sermons. He revered
Mynster as his father's pastor, and his own. Mynster died in
January of 1854; five years earlier in 1849, S.K. wrote in
his journals:

> Sometimes I am almost afraid for the man when I think of
> Bishop Mynster. He is now 72 and soon he will go to his judg-
> ment. And what has he not done to harm Christianity by con-
> juring up a lying picture—so that he could sit back and rule.
> His sermons are quite good—but in eternity he will not have to
> preach—but be judged.[3]

Kierkegaard maintained a public silence, however. When Mynster died, Professor Hans L. Martensen, who had helped introduce the philosophy of Hegel into Denmark, became the new bishop. Martensen, in accepting his new position, spoke of his predecessor, Bishop Mynster, as a "witness to the truth." This was too much. Kierkegaard could be silent no longer. He chose a popular political journal, *The Fatherland,* in which to launch an attack which shocked— and shook—the established Danish Church. The attack was continued in a series of papers called *The Instant;* the entire series of papers has been brought together in a book entitled *Attack Upon Christendom.*

Two things should be made clear at the outset. First, this attack was mounted from *within* the church. In this respect it is similar to the recent "death of God" theology, which also was not just a case of a group of atheists attacking the church, but rather of a group of churchmen, who felt that their church was in need of reform.

The second point is that Kierkegaard's attack was upon "Christendom," not Christianity. S.K. was not arguing against the teachings of Jesus Christ as they are found in the New Testament. Rather, he insisted that these teachings had been abandoned in Christendom as he saw it in the Danish Lutheran Church. As Kierkegaard read his New Testament, an individual may decide to become a Christian. The person must understand that he will have to suffer for his faith. He will be hated by the world; he will live in poverty, and so on. But in the Danish Church, everyone becomes a Christian as a matter of course, just by being born into the state of Denmark; it's automatic. As for the preachers, they are state officials, and, far from being poverty-stricken, they live very well. They wear robes trimmed in velvet, live in fine homes, marry and have families, are paid (well paid) from state funds and enjoy steady promotions. Whatever else this may be, S.K. argued, it is most certainly *not* the Christianity of the New Testament.

Mynster was not, then, a "witness to the truth" of the New Testament. Neither, for that matter, was his successor, Professor Martensen. Kierkegaard also attacked N. F. S. Grundtvig. The reader may not recognize that last name; Grundtvig was a noted writer of hymns, including my favorite, "Built on the Rock." The attack went beyond personalities, of course; it was directed against the church. The substance of the quarrel is summed up in the *Journals,* in a passage S.K. called "The Domestic Goose: a moral tale." S.K. tells us of a group of geese who went to church to worship together each Sunday:

> The sermon was essentially the same each time—it told of the glorious destiny of geese, of the noble end for which their maker had created them—and every time his name was mentioned all of the geese curtsied and all the ganders bowed their heads. They were to use their wings to fly away to the distant pastures to which they really belonged; for they were only pilgrims on this earth.[4]

None of the geese really took this talk about flying seriously, of course. They had long since ceased to be able to fly because they were so well fed by the farmer. They grew fat, too fat for flying. Indeed, the few who refused to eat so much and who worked at exercising their wings—in short, who took their divine mission of flying seriously— were looked upon as freaks, dangerous fanatics. We are not surprised when S.K. adds, "And the same is true of divine worship in Christianity."[5]

The attack, as it appears in the *Attack Upon Christendom,* is much more bitter in tone. I quote only one example:

> This has to be said: by ceasing to take part in the official worship of God as it now is (if in fact thou dost take part in it) thou hast one guilt the less, and that a great one: thou dost not take part in treating God as a fool.[6]

The last paper in Kierkegaard's *Attack* was found on his desk, complete and ready for publication, when he was taken to the hospital October 2, 1855. He died in the midst of the uproar, certainly a "witness to the truth" as he saw it.

The attack on Bishop Mynster and his church may sound familiar to the reader. Something very like it happened again in our century. When Pope Pius XII died in 1958, his fellow Roman Catholics praised him as a great pope. It almost appeared that the Church was ready to proclaim him a saint at once. One man cried out in protest—Rolf Hochhuth. He wrote a play, *The Deputy,* in which he pointed out that Pope Pius XII had been pope during World War II, and had not protested the murder of six million Jews in Hitler's Nazi Germany. In one scene, a young priest has an audience with the Pope and pleads that a letter be sent to Hitler, protesting the Jewish persecution. The Pope refuses, insisting that the Church must remain neutral.

> We cannot—will not—write to Hitler. He would—and in his accursed self the Germans in Corpore—only be antagonized and outraged. But we desire them, and Roosevelt, to see in us impartial go-betweens. Now that is enough. *Ad acta.*[7]

The text of *The Deputy* begins with a number of short epigraphs; one of them is from Kierkegaard's *Attack Upon Christendom.*

Hochhuth was not *quite* alone in his protest. Walter Kaufmann also remembered and wrote in his book *Religion from Tolstoy to Camus:*

> After the war, the Pope took a far stronger stand against Communism than he had ever taken against Nazism. In 1946, for example, he excommunicated Marshal Tito. . . . No such action had been taken against Hitler, Goebbels, and other leading Nazis who were nominal Catholics.[8]

He then added that before he became pope, as Cardinal Pacelli, papal Secretary of State, this man who was to become Pius XII, ". . . had negotiated a concordat with Hitler which required Catholic priests in Germany to swear loyalty to Hitler." [9]

This reference to the Pope's alleged support of Nazism parallels one of Kierkegaard's persistent complaints. Under the Danish law of his day, the state permitted houses of prostitution to continue to exist—provided only that these houses were operated by Christians! [10] Thus, he claimed, the Danish Lutheran Church supported prostitution; it simply made it *Christian* prostitution.

Kierkegaard having died in the midst of this attack upon "Christendom," our biographical statement is completed. To know the man Kierkegaard, we need to study his work, and this will be done in subsequent chapters. But there is another way that we can gain insight into the character and personality of this interesting man. When I meet a man of letters and visit his home, I like to browse through his library to see what books he buys and reads. S.K. had, because of his father's success in business, ample means to buy books. He had a fine library of some 2197 books, and fortunately, we have information regarding that library.[11] Ronald Gregor

Smith tells us there was little or nothing concerning natural science, comparative religion, or pure history in S.K.'s library. But the library was rich in religious and philosophical writings. He had many Bibles in several languages (including the originals, of course). He had a forty-volume set of the works of the church fathers, and much church history. His philosophical works were primarily Greek and recent German. He seems to have been especially interested in Hegel, Socrates (as we know from S.K.'s own work), Spinoza, Schopenhauer, and Trendelenberg. He also had copies of Kant's *Critique of Pure Reason* and *Critique of Judgment*. He had *no* British philosophy at all.

He did have British literature in translation, and was particularly well read in the German translation of Shakespeare's plays. His collection of Danish and German literature was larger. He also enjoyed folk tales, legends, and fairy tales (as a child he had been a schoolmate of Hans Christian Andersen) and we find these imaginative writings frequently reflected in his work.

An examination of Kierkegaard's work reveals that he was not at all interested in setting forth a system. As we shall see, Hegel, the major philosopher of Kierkegaard's day, had a system, and S.K. certainly did not want to imitate him. He was concerned with helping people become Christians. Thus he tried to show that there are a limited number of ways a person can lead his life—and every existing individual must choose from among these.

Briefly, Kierkegaard thought there were three ways that a person could live his life. He spoke of these as the three spheres of existence. Unfortunately, he also sometimes (rarely) spoke of these as *stages*, as in the title of his book, *Stages on Life's Way*, and this can be misleading. *Stages*

suggests a sort of inevitable progress, as in the stages of
growth from childhood to maturity, and one *stage* is left
behind as we move to the next. But neither of these things
is true of S.K.'s spheres. And he *did* more often use the
word *spheres*. So there are spheres of existence, which
Kierkegaard designated, respectively, the *aesthetic* sphere,
the *ethical* sphere, and the *religious* sphere. Since the three
spheres of existence constitute the heart of Kierkegaard's
thought, each in turn will be given rather detailed scrutiny
in the chapters that follow.

II. The Aesthetic Sphere and the Reply to Hegel

THE SEDUCER AND BOREDOM

Kierkegaard's works contain two descriptions of the aesthetic sphere. The first is to be found in his *Either/Or*, the second in his *Stages on Life's Way*. Principally because of its greater clarity, I shall concentrate on the former.

Either/Or is a large book, usually published in two volumes. This may account for the fact that most students of Kierkegaard fail to read the entire book, preferring to partake of selections such as those found in Bretall's *Kierkegaard Anthology*.

For some reason *Either/Or* was published pseudonymously under the name of Victor Eremita. But in the preface to the first volume, Victor Eremita claims not to be the author of the book, only its editor. He (i.e., Victor Eremita) claims to have found the papers that he subsequently published in book form. The papers were supposedly written by two other men. The first set of papers is held to be the work of a young

man, variously called "the Seducer," or simply "A." The
second set is supposedly the work of an older man, "the
Judge," or simply "B." "A's" papers make up the first
volume, "B's" the second, with "A" representing the aesthetic
sphere, "B" the ethical sphere. The entire first volume of
Either/Or is nothing more than an extended character essay,
depicting the life of the aesthetic man.

The first observation to be made about the aesthetic man
is that he constantly seeks pleasure. And, if the reader fails
to notice this, Kierkegaard has Victor Eremita inform us.
Of "A" he says, ". . . his whole life was motivated by
enjoyment." [1]

Surprisingly, perhaps—given the fact that "A" is a
constant seeker after enjoyment—Kierkegaard soon shows
us that the Seducer's life is not a happy one. The very first
section of volume 1, entitled the "Diapsalmata," contains
several short, pithy, admittedly witty, but very cynical bits
of what the Seducer apparently intended to be wisdom. But
it is a sad wisdom:

> Life has become a bitter drink to me and yet I must take it
> like medicine, slowly, drop by drop.[2]
> My life is absolutely meaningless.[3]
> The result of my life is simply nothing, a mood, a single
> colour.[4]
> This life is topsy-turvy and terrible, not to be endured.[5]
> To be a perfect man is after all the highest human ideal. Now
> I have got corns, which ought to help some.[6]
> Even pain has lost its refreshment for me.[7]

Why is the Seducer unhappy? The fact seems to be that
he is simply bored with it all. One of the papers of "A,"
"The Rotation Method," is quite clear on this point. It begins
with a classic account of boredom from Aristophanes'
Plutus:

Chremylos:	You get too much at last of everything, of love,			
Karion:	of bread,			
Chremylos:		of music,		
Karion:			and of sweetmeats.	
Chremylos:	of honor,			
Karion:		cakes,		
Chremylos:			of courage,	
Karion:				and of figs.
Chremylos:	Ambition,			
Karion:		barley-cakes,		
Chremylos:			high office,	
Karion:				lentils.[8]

A single sentence at the beginning of this essay sums up the whole point: "Boredom is the root of all evil." [9]

The Seducer follows his inclinations, and we have seen that he is unhappy and bored. A further point: the Seducer wishes to avoid becoming involved or becoming entangled in any situation that would prevent his freely following his inclinations. Thus "A" says of marriage:

One must always take care not to enter into any relationship in which there is a possibility of many members. For this reason friendship is dangerous, to say nothing of marriage. Husband and wife are indeed said to be one but this is a very dark and mystic saying. When you are one of several, then you have lost your freedom; you cannot send for your traveling boots whenever you wish, you cannot move aimlessly about in the world. If you have a wife it is difficult; if you have a wife and perhaps a child it is troublesome; if you have a wife and children it is impossible. . . . Friendship is dangerous, marriage still more so; for woman is and ever will be the ruin of a man as soon as he contracts a permanent relation with her.[10]

Throughout much of *Either/Or*, volume 1, "A" is concerned with a practical problem, the problem of deciding what sort of seducer to become. In a section entitled "The

Immediate Stages of the Erotic," "A" weighs the possibilities
—the merely sensuous seducer versus the intellectual
seducer. In "A's" ponderings, Mozart's Don Juan represents
the sensuous seducer while Goethe's Faust represents the
intellectual seducer. "A" writes:

> There is evidently something very profound here, which has
> perhaps escaped the attention of most people in that Faust, who
> reproduces Don Juan, seduces only one girl, while Don Juan
> seduces hundreds; but this one girl is also, in an intensive sense,
> seduced and crushed quite differently from all those Don Juan
> had deceived, simply because Faust, as reproduction, falls under
> the category of the intellectual. The power of such a seducer is
> speech, i.e., the lie. . . . Such a seducer is of quite a different
> sort from Don Juan, is essentially different from him . . . and
> from the aesthetic standpoint comes within the category of the
> interesting. The object of his desire is accordingly, when one
> considers him aesthetically, something more than the merely
> sensuous. But what is this force, then, by which Don Juan
> seduces? It is desire, the energy of sensuous desire.[11]

It is worth noting (and I shall return to this point later)
that, when we are permitted to see the Seducer in action in
"The Diary of the Seducer" in volume 1 of *Either/Or*, he
resembles *both* Faust and Don Juan. Thus "A" says of the
Seducer (who, as I shall presently show, is "A" himself):

> He lived far too intellectually to be a seducer in the common
> understanding of the word. Sometimes, however, he assumed
> a parasitic body, and was then sheer sensuality.[12]

A clarification is needed here. The last quotation was
taken from a short preface, by "A," to "The Diary of the
Seducer." "A" claims to have found the diary and does not
admit having written it. It is surprising that so many readers,
including apparently Robert Bretall,[13] have fallen for this

deception. Kierkegaard makes it clear in his (or Victor Eremita's) preface that "A" is the author of all the papers in the first volume as he writes:

> The last of "A's" papers is a story entitled "Diary of the Seducer." Here we meet with new difficulties since "A" does not acknowledge himself as author but only as editor. This is an old trick of the novelist, and I should not object to it, if it did not make my own position so complicated, as one author seems to be enclosed in another like the parts in a Chinese puzzle box. Here is not the place to explain in greater detail the reasons for my opinion. I shall only note that the dominant mood in "A's" preface in a manner betrays the poet.[14]

The humor of the "Chinese puzzle box" is heightened when we realize that in the preface to the Diary, "A" chooses to hide behind the pseudonym of Johannes the Seducer in precisely the same way that Kierkegaard himself hides behind the pseudonym of Victor Eremita in the Preface of *Either/Or*.

A second clarification should also be made. The reader may object to the fact that I have apparently assumed that "sensuousness" and "sensuality" are synonyms since I ignored the usual distinction and let Faust represent sensuousness in one instance and sensuality in another. In English, of course, *sensual* implies moral censure while *sensuous* does not. But, as the translator Walter Lowrie informs us,[15] no such distinction exists in the Danish language. *Sandselig* is forced to do double duty meaning both "sensual" and "sensuous." *Sensuous* is chosen by Lowrie to refer to Don Juan because he (Lowrie) doubts that "A" would have wished to censure a fellow seducer,[16] but it is difficult to understand why Lowrie chose *sensuality* in the preface to the Diary since it would seem that the same consideration would

apply in this second case. Lowrie admits that there were
"times when the translator hasn't known *which* to use." [17]

To return to the description of the Seducer in action, I said
that he is sensuous and yet intellectual. There are passages
in the Diary in which this sensuousness is emphasized; the
Seducer is aroused by the beauty of Cordelia, the girl he
plans to seduce:

> She loosened a little scarf that was fastened about her neck
> under her shawl; a soft breeze from the water fanned her bosom,
> white as snow, and yet warm and full.[18]
>
> How healthily full her lips were! Never have I seen prettier
> ones.[19]

At other times the Seducer is a thinker, calculating,
planning every move:

> One should always make preliminary studies, everything must
> be properly planned.[20]
>
> Consequently, the strategic principle, the law governing every
> move in this campaign, is always to work her into an interesting
> situation. The interesting is the field on which the battle must be
> waged; the potentialities of the interesting must be exhausted.[21]

There are yet other passages in which the Seducer
continues to weigh the sensuous against the intellectual. At
times the intellectual is clearly preferred over the sensuous:
"I simply do not care to possess a girl in the mere external
sense, but to enjoy her in an artistic sense." [22] At other times
the sensuous seems to be preferred: "Enjoy, do not talk.
The people who make a business of such deliberations do
not usually enjoy." [23]

After all these plans and deliberations, the reader may
wonder about the outcome of the seduction attempt. The

Diary has little to say about the seduction itself. We assume that Cordelia was seduced, but it is difficult to be certain even about that. As "A" (who, again, is in fact the Seducer himself) says in the preface to the Diary:

> . . . his affair with Cordelia is so complicated that it was possible for him to appear as the one seduced; indeed even the unfortunate girl herself was sometimes bewildered about it; here, too, his footprints are so indistinct that any certainty is impossible.[24]

The Seducer has done a great deal of planning and calculating, but to what end? There seems to be a great deal of merit in the remark of "B," the ethical man of *Either/Or*, volume 2, who says of "A," "Your life is wholly given over to preliminary runs." [25]

At this point the reader may object that this paradigm of the aesthetic life, as found in *Either/Or*, volume 1, is, perhaps, very interesting from a psychological point of view, but its religious or philosophical significance is less than obvious. The significance of this character essay, as I would classify it, is not clarified in volume 1 of *Either/Or*. For this clarification we must turn to the papers of "B" in volume 2, in which "B" criticizes the aesthetic life of "A."

In view of the fact that "B" represents the ethical life and "A" is a seducer, "B" might be expected to condemn "A" as bad or evil. But "B" does not do this. The point is not that "A" is bad; the point is rather that "A" is not *anything*. As "B" says, "In fact you are nothing." [26] The Seducer is not condemned for having chosen evil rather than good; the fact is that he has not chosen at all.

Thus "B" writes:

> My either/or does not in the first instance denote the choice

between good and evil; it denotes the choice whereby one chooses good *and* evil or excludes them. Here the question is under what determinants one would contemplate the whole of existence and would himself live. That the man who chooses good and evil chooses the good is indeed true, but this becomes evident only afterwards; for the aesthetical is not evil but neutrality, and that is the reason why I affirmed that it is the ethical which constitutes the choice. It is, therefore, not so much a question of choosing between willing the good or the evil, as of choosing to will, but by this in turn the good and the evil are posited.[27]

Someone may object that the aesthetic man *does* choose. He must choose because he acts, and surely there is a sense in which one can say that the fact that one acts in a certain way is proof that he chose to act in that way. S.K. recognizes this:

The aesthetic choice is either entirely immediate and to that extent no choice, or it loses itself in the multifarious. Thus, when a young girl follows the choice of her heart, this choice, however beautiful it may be, is in the strictest sense no choice, since it is entirely immediate.[28]

Here Kierkegaard seems to mean that when she simply follows her inclinations (as the aesthetic man does) rather than weighing alternatives and making a decision between or among these alternatives, this simply will not count as a choice "in the strictest sense."

But what does Kierkegaard mean when he says that the aesthetic choice is either immediate—simply following one's inclinations (as explained above) or "loses itself in the multifarious"? "B's" papers contain a lengthy, and, I consider, important example in which "B" depicts "A" trying to choose a profession:

Yea, if to deliberate were the proper task for a human life, you would be pretty close to perfection. I will adduce an example. To fit your case the contrasts must be bold: either a parson/or an actor. Here is the dilemma. Now all your passionate energy is awakened, reflection with its hundred arms lays hold of the thought of being a parson. You find no repose, day and night you think about it, you read all the books you can lay your hands on, you go to church three times every Sunday, pick up acquaintance with parsons, write sermons yourself, deliver them to yourself; for half a year you are dead to the whole world. You can now talk of the clerical calling with more insight and apparently with more experience than many who have been parsons for twenty years. When you encounter such men it arouses your indignation that they do not know how to get the thing off their chests with more eloquence. "Is this enthusiasm?" you say, "Why I who am not a parson, who have not consecrated myself to this calling, speak with the voice of angels as compared with them." That, perhaps, is true enough, but nevertheless you have not become a parson. Then you act in the same way with respect to the other task, and your enthusiasm for art almost surpasses your clerical eloquence. Then you are ready to choose. However, one may be sure that in the prodigious thought-production you were engaged in there must have been lots of wasteproducts, many incidental reflections and observations. Hence, the instant you have to choose, life and animation enter into this waste mass, a new either/or presents itself—jurist, perhaps advocate, this has something in common with both the other alternatives. Now you are lost. For that same moment you are at once advocate enough to be able to prove the reasonableness of taking a third possibility into account. So your life drifts on.[29]

The above is a clear example of the aesthetic choice which "loses itself in the multifarious" so that no real choice is ever made. This example closely resembles "A's" trying to choose between the intellectual and sensuous seducer in volume 1. In both cases the contrasting possibilities are retained (no decisive choice is made between them) in a higher unity. The seducer is finally both sensuous and intel-

lectual, but the seduction is so complicated that one wonders
if he really became anything; the end of volume 1 finds him
still deliberating.

In the above example, neither of the contrasting possibilities is chosen and a new possibility arises which "has
something in common with both alternatives." And then yet
another possibility arises in contrast with this new one, and
so on and so on. These examples of the seducer trying to
decide between becoming sensuous or intellectual and, in
this later example, of deciding between becoming a parson
or an actor are valuable clues in the attempt to discover the
philosophical and religious significance of Kierkegaard's
description of the aesthetic life. S.K. describes his purpose
in a perfectly unambiguous way when he has "B" say:

> For the polemical result which resounds in all your songs of
> triumph over life has a strange resemblance to the pet theory
> of the newer philosophy, that the principle of contradiction is
> annulled. . . . As soon as one would transport philosophy into the
> practical domain it must reach the same result you reach.[30]

"THE PHILOSOPHER OF OUR DAY"
—KANT AND HEGEL

It now becomes clear that Kierkegaard's description of
the aesthetic life is his criticism of Hegel, for it was Hegel
who taught that the principle of contradiction is *only
partially* true. There is also identity in the diversity of
opposites; reason can unite (Hegel's term was *aufheben*)
opposites in a higher unity that somehow partakes of both.[31]

The most difficult task of this book is to set forth, in a
clear way, the main outlines of Hegel's philosophy, so that
the reader may see the point of S.K.'s criticisms. Unfortu-

nately, to understand Kierkegaard's response to Hegel we must look back beyond Hegel to Kant, and even back beyond Kant. In the exposition that follows, I shall attempt to be brief. Brief explanations of complex philosophical systems are always oversimplifications, but I think that the following is substantially accurate.

Immanuel Kant (1724–1804) was the greatest German philosopher, and one of the great thinkers of all time, of any country or age. He sought to unify the warring factions of Rationalism and Empiricism. Roughly, the Empiricists (e.g., Locke, Berkeley, and Hume) taught that all knowledge comes to us through sense experience. They thought of the mind as passive, simply receiving and cataloging sense impressions. The Empiricists had trouble finding a place in their systems for such abstract notions as the cause and effect relation, and space and time. On the other hand, the Rationalists (e.g., Descartes, Leibniz, and Spinoza) taught that knowledge comes to us through the use of our minds, i.e., through rational activity, through reason.

Kant decided that both groups were wrong. In his major work on the theory of knowledge, *The Critique of Pure Reason*—and remember Kierkegaard owned a copy of this book—Kant summed up his opposition to both groups in the oft-quoted line, "Thoughts without content are empty, intuitions without concepts are blind." [32] By this he meant that we receive an immense amount of data through our senses, which data is then sorted, arranged, "made *sense* of," by our minds. To cite a common example, think of hearing a melody. What is required to hear a melody? To hear a melody requires the use of our minds because we have no melody (but only disconnected notes) unless we can, in a sense, hear the notes all at once. We must hold the notes in our mind, compare them, see how they are related, in short, how they fit together to make a melody. On the other hand we clearly cannot hear a melody unless we *hear* the notes; the sense of hearing is required. So it is with all of our knowledge; the mind receives the data and then acts upon it. Kant agreed with the Empiricists that sense perceptions are necessary for knowledge; otherwise, he argued, the mind would lack data (and thus would be "empty") upon which to act. But the active agency of the mind is needed, too. A chaos of unsorted data is, Kant said, "blind"; it cannot constitute knowledge, either—and in this he agreed with the Rationalists.

Two other points must be added before we leave Kant. First, he argued that we can know only what our senses tell us, and the way that things are arranged by our minds. He distinguished between things as they appear to us (or phenomena) and things as they really are. He spoke of the *Ding an sich* (or "thing in itself") as being unknowable; in other words, no possible experience could assure us that things really are as we experience them. Second, he could not prove the *existence* of space and time and the causal relation; perhaps these are only part of the "furniture of our minds," the way our minds sort things out. Human beings do see things as causally ordered in space and time. But it is extremely important, for an understanding of Kant, that this may simply be the way we experience things. When the Bible tells us (2 Pet. 3:8) ". . . that one day is with the Lord as a thousand years, and a thousand years as one day," this may mean that God does not experience things in that way. Again, we can never be sure that things are really as we experience them.

Thus there is a persistent skepticism pervading the philosophy of Kant, and it was in response to this that Hegel formulated his philosophical system. George William Frederick Hegel (1770–1831) was unquestionably *the* most important intellectual figure of the nineteenth century, as the fact that his work led to the dialectical materialism of Karl Marx amply demonstrates. But we can also point to Hegelians and neo-Hegelians in the nineteenth and twentieth centuries, such as F. H. Bradley and T. H. Green and Bernard Bosanquet in England, Benedetto Croce in Italy and Josiah Royce (Harvard University) and Radaslav Tsanoff (Rice University) in our own country. His influence was, and is, enormous. We have already noted that Professor Martensen and other scholars had introduced Hegel's thought into Kierkegaard's Denmark. But this does not tell us what Hegel taught, and to that we must turn.

In response to Kant, Hegel argued that there is no reason to postulate a *Ding an sich* which is forever unknowable. Why not assume that things are as we know them, as we experience them, and (more importantly) as our minds arrange things? To Kant's question "How can we know—how could we *prove* that things *are* as arranged by our minds?" Hegel replied, "Of course, we *can't* ever prove it, but why assume otherwise?" What was new and daring about Hegel's philosophy was the suggestion that *if* reality corresponds to the way our minds work, we could best study reality by studying the way our minds work, that is, by studying the way we understand things. Our reason *does* reveal reality to us, he insisted, and if our reason ever failed us, what extrarational power have we to correct it?

How do our minds understand things then? Consider a simple example. We say that a triangle is a three-sided plane figure. This means to understand what it is to be three-sided;

the figure has three-sidedness. It has the characteristic of being a plane figure, rather than a solid, as a sphere or a cylinder. To understand the notion of a triangle, then, is to understand the characteristics, which we could call universals or *essences*, which make up the concept.

Hegel thought it was just that way, only more complicated, with everything. His system is made up of these universals or essences, which he thought were logically related. Briefly, he thought that to grasp an essence involves thinking, too, of its opposite. But then we see that the opposites are not really contradictions, but have something in common. They can be resolved in a higher unity which partakes of both, a new universal which resolves the contradiction. This, in what I realize is a vastly oversimplified form, is the Hegelian dialectic.

But we need to emphasize two major points, whether or not we can (and I doubt that *anyone* can) fully understand Hegel. First, Hegel's system is a system of thought; it is concerned with understanding reality. Second, the system is made up of universals. What happens again, is that we want to understand reality, so we contemplate the universals that comprise whatever it is we wish to understand. It turns out, Hegel thought, that we will see that the universals are logically related in such a way that what are at first thought opposites are found to have much in common, and at last are resolved in a higher unity.

In direct opposition to Hegel's philosophy Kierkegaard wrote his *Either/Or*, summing his argument all up neatly in a passage in which "the Judge," the ethical man of volume 2 of *Either/Or*, criticizes the young seducer:

If you are asked whether you will sign your name to an address to the King, or whether you desire a constitution or the right to impose taxes, or whether you will join this or that benevolent movement, you reply, "My revered contemporary, you misunderstand me, I am not in the game at all, I am outside. . . ." So it is with the philosopher, he is outside, he is not in the game, he sits and grows old listening to the songs of long ago, harkening to the harmonies of mediation. I honor science, I respect its devotees, but life, too, has its demands.[33]

The point, simply stated, is that Hegel's philosophy was concerned with knowing, not with doing. But ethical and religious matters call not simply for knowledge, but for action. We must realize that we are involved and have choices which we have to make. Remember that the Seducer is S.K.'s example of the aesthetic life. Why this word *aesthetic?* William Barrett tells us that "the word 'aesthetic' comes from the Greek verb meaning to sense or perceive; it has the same root as the word 'theory' and the word 'theatre'." [34] At a theater we do not dash onstage in defense of the heroine, or shout, "Don't drink it, it's poisoned!" when she seems to be in danger. We are only spectators, not involved, "not in the game," but outside. The theoretical philosopher can also be a spectator of life. He spins his theories, juggles universals, but never *does* anything. He sees the various alternatives as possibilities for thought. As Barrett also says (and Kierkegaard) some of these possibilities are interesting and some are boring, but the aesthetic man never sees these alternatives as more than that. This is why "B" said of him, as indicated earlier, "In fact you are nothing." The aesthetic man is neither good nor bad, strictly speaking, in moral terms; he simply never sees that a choice has to be made.

Consider a simple example. I happen to be a philosophy professor, and I sometimes teach ethics, or moral theory. Suppose a young lady in my ethics class drops by the office to speak to me. It's obvious that she's worried, distraught, and has been crying. Finally, she blurts out, "I love this boy, and now he's about to be drafted. He wants me to spend the weekend in a motel with him. Would this be wrong? Tell me what I ought to do." The sad truth is that too often we reply to such an outcry by saying, "I'm not in the game at all, I'm outside." Today we might, in the tradition of British Analytic philosophy, reply by saying, "Well, much depends on what you mean by *wrong*, and that's a word with many meanings; *ought* is also extremely difficult to analyze . . ." etc., etc. Kierkegaard interpreted the Hegelian philosopher as saying that apparently a seduction is involved here, and there are various types of seducers (Don Juan, Faust, etc.), and probably different types of seductions, too; and much could be said about that. . . . But finally the poor girl might interrupt, "Listen, he means *tonight!*" She has to decide, but the aesthetic man does not see this. At one point S.K. wrote,

> Hence in our age as the order of the day we have the disgusting sight of young men who are able to mediate Christianity and paganism . . . and are unable to tell a plain man what he has to do in life, and do not know any better what they themselves have to do.[35]

It is recorded that Hegel himself was forced to move to South Germany by the Battle of Jena. But he was never made to feel personally involved. He did not become patriotic, or angry, or anything, apparently. The Danish historian Höffding remarked that Hegel "felt himself a spectator only . . . whose only concern was to find a quiet corner for himself." [36]

In this one instance at least, Hegel himself was a perfect example of what Kierkegaard called the aesthetic man.

It should be apparent by now that the portrait drawn in volume 1 of *Either/Or* of the aesthetic man is intended as a criticism of the Hegelian philosophy. More ramifications and implications were developed by Kierkegaard, but are not needed for discussion here. The main criticism, once more, is that the aesthetic man does not see that he must be *involved*, that he must make moral or religious choices.

Kierkegaard said it better than any of his commentators, as he said of Hegel's philosophy:

> In relation to their systems most systematisers are like a man who builds an enormous castle and lives in a shack nearby; they do not live in their own enormous systematic buildings. But spiritually that is a decisive objection. Spiritually speaking a man's thought must be the building in which he lives—otherwise everything is topsy-turvy.[37]

JEAN-PAUL SARTRE AND EXISTENTIALISM

Largely because of his criticisms of Hegel, Kierkegaard is often called the first existentialist, the founder of existentialism. Because good definitions of "existentialism" are hard to find and many philosophers are called existentialists who seem to have very little in common, we need more insight here. Probably the best-known existential philosopher today is the French atheistic thinker Jean-Paul Sartre (b. 1905). Sartre is recognized by most philosophers as a paradigm of what "existentialism" means. We can, therefore, determine what it means to call Kierkegaard an existentialist if we know something about Sartre, and then make comparisons and contrasts.[38]

Sartre's most important book, *Being and Nothingness* (published in 1943, translated by Hazel Barnes and published in English in 1956), has the subtitle *An Essay on Phenomenological Ontology*. If we can understand what is meant by "phenomenological ontology," we have probably understood Sartre's central teachings. In classical philosophy ontology was the study of Being. Sartre begins by dividing all of Being, i.e., everything that is, into two groups— *Être en soi* and *Être pour soi* ("Being in itself" and "Being for itself"). The terms are frightening but the distinction is simple. The *pour soi* is conscious being; the *en soi* is unconscious (or nonconscious) being. Rocks and trees are not conscious, thus *en soi*; people are conscious, thus *pour soi*. The difference thus becomes the difference between people and things. Most of Sartre's philosophy can be understood in terms of a series of propositions about these two classes of Being. Of the *Être en soi*, Being-in-itself, he says:

I. "It is what it is." [39]

By this curious expression, Sartre means that things have a certain stability. An oak tree, to use one of Sartre's favorite examples, is an oak tree. It's not likely to become anything else. It cannot become an apple tree, or a pig, or a string of pearls, or anything else. If it is cut down, the remains will be oak; if burned, the ashes—oak ashes. To say that it is an oak tree sums up its very essence; that's what it *is*. This stability intrigues the characters in Sartre's novels and plays; for example, it is the point of Antoine's remark, "Stones are hard and do not move." [40]

II. It is what it appears to be.

This explains the sense in which Sartre's ontology is

phenomenological. As we have observed, Kant, in the *Critique of Pure Reason*, said that we could only know things as they appear to us, and these appearances he called "phenomena." But Kant thought it possible that things as they really are might be other than as we see them. He thus postulated a *Ding an sich* or thing-in-itself which is inaccessible to mere human perception. Even though he thought we could know only phenomena, he also thought we may be cheated; there may be more—the *Ding an sich*—which forever escapes us.

Sartre's reaction was quite different from Hegel's. Sartre sees no reason to postulate a *Ding an sich* and boldly asserts that the world of appearances is the only world: "Now I knew; things are entirely what they appear to be—and behind them . . . there is nothing." [41]

III. It is not exhausted in its appearing.

An extended quote may suffice here better than any explanation. In *Nausea*, Antoine looks at a black root at his feet:

> The simplest, most indefinable quality had too much content, in relation to itself, in its heart. That black against my feet, it didn't look like black, but rather the confused effort to imagine black by someone who had never seen black and who wouldn't know how to stop, who would have imagined an ambiguous being beyond colours. It *looked like* a colour but also . . . like a bruise or a secretion, like an oozing and something else, an odour, for example, it melted into the odour of wet earth, warm, moist wood, in a flavour of chewed, sweet fibre. I did not simply see this black; sight is an abstract invention, a simplified idea, one of man's ideas. That black, amorphous, weakly presence, far surpassed sight, smell and taste. But this richness was lost in confusion and finally was no more because it was too much. [42]

Nothing can be completely known because it can never be

completely experienced. To know anything completely would
be to see it, hear it, touch it, etc., under all possible conditions.

An example from art may be helpful. The French Im-
pressionist Monet painted a number of canvases of the
Rouen Cathedral, seen under different lighting conditions.
A recent book on modern painting reproduces one of these
canvases and adds a note:

> He shows the Cathedral at dawn, at noon, at dusk, in bright and
> grey weather, in a transparent atmosphere or in a mist. However,
> if each time he discovered a new aspect of the Cathedral, always
> there is one essential missing, its consistency. By dint of exam-
> ining only one aspect of reality, Monet ended by depriving
> objects of their solidity, their weight and their matter; so his
> subjects tend to become unreal.[43]

This commentary suggests that Monet should have shown
us the cathedral as it *really* is, but it's just possible that
Monet, like Sartre, wanted to show us that our most complete knowledge of the cathedral is gained by seeing it, again
and again, under as many different conditions as possible.

So much for the *en soi*. What Sartre says of the *pour soi*
is best understood in contrast with this. Of the *pour soi*,
conscious being, or people, Sartre says:

I. "It . . . is not what it is." [44]

A man never is anything, once and for all, until he dies,
and then he is what he has done. While an oak tree *is* an
oak tree, I am not a teacher in that sense. I may cease to
be a teacher tomorrow and become something entirely different. The reason is that:

II. Man is free.

A man does not become something in the same way that acorns become oak trees. A man becomes what he becomes through his own free choice. Sartre's short story "The Wall" [45] shows the extent to which he believes in freedom. The story tells of a fighter in the Spanish Revolution who is captured and then told that he will be shot if he does not tell where his leader is hiding. Finally, in an ironic ending, the revolutionary decides to invent the wild tale that his leader is hiding in the cemetery. It turns out the leader *did* hide there, so he was shot and the prisoner was released. But the point remains; even when faced with the wall, a man is free. This freedom is a mixed blessing, however, because:

III. A man cannot renounce his freedom.

We are not free not to be free. This is a key to Sartre's psychology. Man yearns for the stability of the *en soi*, but can never achieve it. This is one of Sartre's main themes and a favorite dramatic device, so examples abound. In *Being and Nothingness* Sartre speaks of a gambler who resolves to stop gambling and who believes in the effectiveness of his resolution. But when he returns to the gaming tables "what he apprehends then in anguish is precisely the total inefficacy of the past resolution." [46] In short, this man was a gambler, which is but to say that he *has gambled*. What this gambler sought to do was become something else (a non-gambler, perhaps). But while "gambler" and "non-gambler" are both possibilities of this man, there is no way that he can permanently make himself into a non-gambler. His resolution, while perhaps fine and noble, is no ironclad guarantee against gambling. Each time he approaches the tables he must once again choose from among his possibilities. He can never relinquish his freedom and become absolutely and for all time one of those possibilities. As Iris Murdoch points out, Sartre feels so strongly the anguish of that fact that one of his characters, Daniel in *Roads to Freedom*, "wishes 'to be a pederast as an oaktree is an oaktree.' Yet he is never able to *experience* a pure coincidence with his vice; he remains detached from it, an observer, a possibility." [47]

Man's great desire is to *be* something once and for all, and yet retain his consciousness. But this is not possible. He would also like to reduce other people to mere things, but he cannot. This is the reason for the continual war that Sartre envisions between each man and every other man. This is why in *No Exit*, a story of three people in Hell, Garcin asserts that "Hell is other people!" [48] Each of us would make the other a *thing*, while retaining our freedom, and becoming something permanent. We seek to be both *en soi* and *pour soi*, but the combination is contradictory. This last passage also explains Sartre's atheism. God, if he existed, would be at once *en soi* and *pour soi*, an impossible combination. [49]

These propositions have far-reaching consequences, explaining the sense in which Sartre is an existentialist. By contrast, the German philosopher, Leibniz, is the perfect example of what Sartre would call an essentialist (and the theologian John Calvin would be just as good an example). For Leibniz (and Calvin), God preordains everything and thus each of us has, in his mind before our birth, an essence which it is our inescapable destiny to realize. For Sartre—and this is often advanced as a definition of existentialism—*man's existence precedes his essence*. [50] Man *is*, before he is anything. He is thrown into the world and becomes whatever he becomes through his own free choice, though he can never become anything once and for all.

The reader will forgive what must seem a lengthy digression. But I have learned by bitter experience that just tossing out the definition "existence precedes essence" doesn't get the job done; we must make sense of it first. Now if this is, as I assume it is, an acceptable definition of existentialism, does Kierkegaard conform to it? Obviously, Kierkegaard would reject Sartre's atheism, probably by simply rejecting the definitions of *en soi* and *pour soi* upon which it is based. But there are many similarities. Kierkegaard rejected the Hegelian system of essences and emphasized existence—life as it is lived—instead. He emphasized *choice* (more on this in the next chapter) as did Sartre. As we shall see in our discussion of the "leap of faith" in chapter 4, Kierkegaard, like Sartre, had an extreme doctrine of freedom. Clearly, if Sartre had been a Christian, his "existence precedes essence" dictum would have led him to reject the once-in-grace-always-in-grace doctrine. Kierkegaard didn't talk about that, so far as I know, but it seems significant that he never spoke of himself as *being* a Christian but only as *becoming* a Christian.

Let us summarize these results. When we call Kierkegaard an existentialist we usually mean only that he stressed life as it is lived, and rejected Hegel's system and its essences. Further, he influenced later writers, such as Sartre, who call themselves existentialists. Candidly, we do not usually have a precise definition of "existentialism" in mind when we call Kierkegaard an existentialist, but if we take Sartre's definition, I think we can argue that Kierkegaard fits it pretty well though there are obvious implications drawn by Sartre, for example, atheism and the war of every man against every other, which Kierkegaard would have rejected.

Now we must return to the exposition of Kierkegaard's thought. Before we digressed, we had begun to discuss moral matters. It is time for a fuller discussion of Kierkegaard's ethical sphere of existence.

III. Ethics Is Not Enough

KIERKEGAARD'S ETHICAL THEORY

One of the very best books on Kierkegaard is *The Mind of Kierkegaard* by the Roman Catholic scholar James Collins. Professor Collins's chapter on Kierkegaard's ethics bears the title "The Ethical View and Its Limits." The title is significant because Kierkegaard was concerned to show that there is a sphere of existence, or way of life, which is higher than the ethical. He is more concerned with showing the *limits* of the ethical life than in simply telling us what the ethical life is like. His account of the ethical life is important, however, because the religious life is outlined by contrast with the ethical.

For our discussion we need to return to Kierkegaard's book *Either/Or*, this time to volume 2. Before considering the content of the book, we should emphasize that the title contains one of Kierkegaard's strongest protests against the Hegelian philosophy. Kierkegaard makes it clear that this disjunction *(Either/Or)* involves exclusive alternatives. The ethical Judge says to the young Seducer at one point, "What I have so often said to you I say now once again, or rather I shout it: Either/Or, *aut/aut.*" [1] This is a rather subtle point. Our English expression *either/or* is ambiguous. Sometimes we say either/or and mean that one alternative is true, perhaps both, as when we say, "The doors of the hospital are open to those who are either injured or diseased." Obviously we would admit people unfortunate enough to be both injured and diseased. But when we say, "In this game we permit no tie scores; you must either win or lose," we mean you can win or lose, but not both. So the English *either/or* is ambiguous.

Latin has two expressions: When we mean at least one, possibly both, the word is *vel;* when we mean at least one and only one of the alternatives is true, the word is *aut.* Thus when S.K. has the Judge say "I shout it: Either/Or, *aut/aut,*" this is a clear protest against Hegel's willingness to accept opposites and mediate them, preserving them in some sort of higher unity. What Kierkegaard is saying is that one must choose between good and evil because the two are different and this difference cannot be mediated.

The first major difference between the ethical and the aesthetic spheres is, then, that the ethical sphere demands a choice, whereas the aesthetic man considers opposites as mere possibilities for thought and does not recognize the necessity of choosing. The ethical Judge devotes a large amount of his writing to this point. Frequently the reference to Hegel is obvious. For example, in an obvious reference to Hegel's logical deduction of the categories, the Judge writes:

But I return to my category. I have only one, for I am not a
logician, but I assure you that it is the choice both of my heart
and of my thought, my soul's delight and my bliss—I return to
the importance of choosing.[2]

We can, however, overemphasize this matter of choosing.
Paul L. Holmer, who has probably done the best work to
date on the subject of Kierkegaard's ethics, goes astray in
suggesting that what mattered for S.K. was choosing, though
what we choose is of no importance. Holmer wrote: "The
nature of ethics—religious truth is such that even after the
correct philosophical account, the ethical issue is left to
the passionate inwardness of each individual." [3] This could
lead the reader to the conclusion that the proper answer to any
question about Kierkegaard's ethical theory is that he had
none. But in fact he did have an ethical theory, as he indicated quite clearly, as he had his ethical Judge say:

Here I might break off, for I have now brought you to the point
where I would have you, that is if you yourself will to be there.
I wanted you to tear yourself loose from the illusions of the
aesthetic life. . . . It is not my intention, however, to break off,
for from this point of vantage I would give you a reflection upon
life, an ethical life view.[4]

The truth is, however, that Kierkegaard did not have a
distinctive ethical theory of his own. He adopted, with
certain adjustments, the ethical theory of Immanuel Kant.
Let us examine S.K.'s theory briefly, emphasizing the details
necessary for an understanding of the later account of the
religious life.

Kierkegaard introduced his ethical "life view" almost
casually:

In opposition to an aesthetical view which would enjoy life, one often hears of another view of life, which finds the significance of life in living for the fulfillment of its duties. With this one intends to indicate an ethical life view.[5]

This passage indicates the Kantian quality of Kierkegaard's ethical theory in two ways. First and most obviously, this ethical theory is concerned with questions of duty (obligation, etc.) and not, or only secondarily, with the question of value, that is, what is the *good* life? Secondly, the life of duty is opposed to the "aesthetic view which would enjoy life," thus introducing the Kantian opposition of duty and inclination.

KANTIAN DUTY AND INCLINATION

Someone once asked, "Why is it that everything I enjoy doing is either sinful, immoral, or fattening?" Sometimes we interpret the statement that duty and inclination are different to mean that if you enjoy something, or are inclined to do it, it must be wrong. Some Christian fundamentalists talk that way. But that was not Kant's point.

Consider an example. Suppose a soldier is given a medal for killing a large number of the enemy, and thus, perhaps, saving his regiment. We would expect the hero to say, "I only did my duty. They attacked my guard post which I was pledged to defend." This would be a good moral reason. But suppose instead our "hero" replied, "I just decided to stand and fight because I enjoy that sort of thing. I like to kill people; it's fun." This would be monstrous. Of course, we *might* enjoy doing what is also our duty, as in the case of giving alms to the poor. Even so, the act is moral, Kant taught, if done from duty, and "I just enjoy it" makes an odd-sounding moral reason. It is to be hoped that we *will* enjoy helping people, but that doesn't make our helping them morally right; it's *right* because it's our duty.

This point bears emphasis because in the argument between the young Seducer and the Judge, the Seducer makes the claim that the life of duty is, and logically *must* be, a life of misery. The Judge takes note of the objections:

> You [i.e., the Seducer] say "Conjugal love conceals in itself something quite different. It seems so mild and heartfelt and tender, but as soon as the door is closed behind the married pair, then before you can say Jack Robinson out comes the rod called duty. You may deck out the scepter as much as you will, you can make it into a Shrovetide rod, it still remains a rod." [6]

Let us be clear. The young Seducer is advocating his own life-style, claiming that real joy in life is found in never marrying, but just seducing every girl that happens to interest you. The Judge's answer to this is one of the best arguments against sexual promiscuity that I have seen, and this is important in our day of "the pill" when it is no longer persuasive to tell our young that they must avoid premarital or extramarital intercourse because of venereal disease or unwanted pregnancies. VD can be cured (though not as simply as many believe) and pregnancy can be avoided. And if the girl does "get caught" and becomes pregnant, abortions are becoming more common—and safer, too— every day.

So what's wrong with "free love"? I think, again, that Kierkegaard's reply is classic. The older Judge is a married man. The first of his papers is called "The Aesthetic Validity of Marriage." It is as if the married Judge is saying, "All right, we can argue in *your* terms." He sets out to show that the moral life, the life of duty exemplified in marriage, rather than seduction, is also more enjoyable than the aesthetic life. The following passage sums things up beautifully:

> Let us then cast up the account once for all. You talk so much about the erotic embrace—what is that in comparison with the matrimonial embrace! What richness of modulation in the matrimonial 'Mine!' in comparison with the erotic! It re-echoes not only in the seductive eternity of the instant, not only in the illusory eternity of fantasy and imagination, but in the eternity of clear consciousness, in the eternity of eternity. What power there is in the matrimonial 'Mine!'—for will, resolution and purpose have a deeper tone.[7]

Kierkegaard saw that the search for pleasure after pleasure does not produce lasting happiness. The life of the Seducer had led to boredom, and the case is not different in our own day. The fact seems to be that the Seducer and many of the young (and sad to say, also their elders) of our day think of sex as one thinks of engaging in some sport, such as football. We practice to become proficient in sports, and gain greater enjoyment from playing the sport well. But the end of this route is boredom, not the happiness we seek. We want more than that. We want ultimately to belong to someone, who also belongs to us, and only marriage can achieve this result. A life of endless seduction cannot; a person who gives himself or herself sexually to everyone never really belongs to anyone.

Continuing the account of Kierkegaard's ethical theory requires considering one example from a Kantian point of view. Suppose a student is taking a test. The student isn't doing too well; he may fail. So he considers cheating on the test. How would Kant argue that he should not? First, Kant would say that if cheating is right for this one student, it must be right for everyone—he took moral laws to be universal truths. So we must ask, what if everyone cheated? If everyone cheated, the test would lose its point; it wouldn't reveal anything about the student's (or the students') ability. So this kind of act, if done by everyone, would be pointless. Kant thought that showed it must be wrong to cheat.[8]

Several things could be emphasized in this example, but only three claim our attention here. First, this way of thinking about ethics is rather abstract. Hegel was not, after all, the first German philosopher to deal in philosophical abstractions. And S.K. found fault with Kant on this score in that he thought Kant's ethic was too abstract.

Second, it is difficult to handle all moral situations in terms of this model. Suppose we ask, where do we get our duties anyway? We can explain our duty to abstain from cheating on exams in terms of this model, and we can adapt this model to our duties to abstain from lying and stealing. But return to the previous example of the soldier defending his guard post. When does the guard get his duties? We know the answer: he has certain duties just because he's a guard. In the U.S. Army, he will be bound by general orders which apply to all guards, and he will have certain special orders which apply to his post. Put somewhat technically, Kierkegaard altered the Kantian ethic to emphasize what we would call self-realization, the view that our duties originate in the roles we play in the social order. We have certain duties as guards or as teachers, and sometimes (as in the case of the guard) these duties are quite formally stated. Less formally, we have certain duties in our role as the

husband or wife of someone, or as father or son. S.K. has
"B," the ethical man, say:

> I perform my duties as a judge assessor, I am glad to have such
> a calling. I believe it is in keeping with my faculties and with
> my whole personality. I know that it makes demands upon my
> powers. I seek to fit myself for it more and more, and in doing
> so I feel that I am developing myself more and more.[9]

THE ETHIC OF SELF-REALIZATION

At the end of the nineteenth century, self-realization was
probably the most popular moral philosophy, and the best
example is undoubtedly the work of the British neo-Hegelian
philosopher F. H. Bradley.[10] But a third general point is
very important for Kierkegaard. From Kant, he accepted
the view that a moral man can always justify himself
rationally. When asked, "Why are you doing that?" a moral
man can *always* cite a universal rule which justifies his
action. When he (i.e., the moral agent) says it is his duty
to refrain from cheating, he can show logically, rationally
why this must be so, as we did above. When asked why he
looks after and protects his son, a father can cite the universal rule that this is what the role of being a father calls for.

A couple of criticisms of Kierkegaard deserve mention
here. He does not seem to have understood that a self-
realization ethic leads to relativism. That is, we may speak
of the duties of a husband, but these will vary from society
to society. In our society, we usually expect a husband to
care for, provide for, look after his wife; but in some
societies the wife does everything for the husband. So the
duties of a husband are not, as S.K. apparently thought,
absolute; they are variable.

Further, there are some roles that we think no one should have. Take the case of Adolf Eichmann, who was alleged to have been responsible for the deaths of six million Jews. To a certain extent we seem to operate in such cases on the basis of the self-realization ethic. When we are told, "I was only a soldier under orders," we can (and properly, too) deny this and insist that soldiers have a duty to fight their nation's enemies, but not to exterminate en masse innocent civilians; this is why Lt. Calley's defense failed. Note, by the way, that we admire such fine soldiers as the Nazi General Rommel. So Eichmann was not just a soldier under orders. But suppose he says, "I was a jailer, in charge of prisoners, and only obeyed my orders." Again we can deny this, saying that it is no part of the proper role of a jailer to destroy, en masse, his prisoners. But now suppose Eichmann said, "Well then, I was Hitler's number one 'Jew-killer'; my job was to destroy all Jews." Now we have to operate in a different way; we want to say that *this* role is a role that no one should have. Clearly, it is difficult to say this on the basis of a self-realization ethic.

These criticisms must not make us forget the main point, which is, once again, that Kierkegaard thought—and here he was heavily influenced by Kant—that a moral man could always provide a rational justification for his action, that he could always appeal to a universal rule which made his action logically right. Thus, if I am a moral man and you ask me, "Why are you doing that?" I can tell you—and convince you if you are rational—that I'm doing the right thing. This is Kierkegaard's account of the ethical sphere. The ethical man, in contrast to the aesthetic man, realizes that life demands that he make choices, *and* he can justify those choices rationally.

THE TELEOLOGICAL SUSPENSION OF THE ETHICAL

Now we must move higher. Kierkegaard argued that there is a sphere of existence, or way of life, higher than the ethical life. In his own terminology, there is a "teleological suspension of the ethical." That is, there is a *telos*, or goal, that is higher than the ethical, in relation to which ethical rules must be suspended, as we go beyond them. This higher life is, of course, the religious life.

The entire argument is based on the biblical story of Abraham and Isaac, as found in Genesis 22. The story is familiar. God spoke to Abraham and commanded him to kill his son, Isaac. Abraham was willing to do this and actually took his son up the mountain, prepared him for sacrifice and was about to take his life when God stayed his hand and provided a ram, which Abraham sacrificed instead. We cannot assume that this was simply a test and that God would never have permitted Isaac to be killed. Remember that Jephthah's daughter was not so lucky (Judges 11); she actually was sacrificed.

How is Abraham's action to be judged? The Bible tells us that "Abraham believed God and it was accounted to him for righteousness" (Gal. 3:6, quoting Gen. 15:6). But, Kierkegaard claimed, he cannot be judged righteous on moral grounds: "Abraham's relation to Isaac, ethically speaking, is quite simply expressed by saying that a father shall love his son more dearly than himself." [11]

As indicated above, the ethical man operates on the basis of universal moral rules, which may be inferred from his social role. We know what fathers should do—love their sons, take care of them, keep them from danger. But Abraham was ready to *kill* his son—how is it possible that he could be righteous? Kierkegaard's answer is, apparently, that Abraham is a justified exception to our moral rules. And, as Jean Wahl has argued, "The justified exception is not justifiable by a rule." [12]

Kierkegaard may have chosen the example of Abraham and Isaac because Kant objected so much to it. Kant believed that, strictly speaking, moral rules can have no exceptions. [13] If a man violates a universal moral rule, he acts wrongly, indefensibly. Thus Kant thought that the story of Abraham and Isaac had to be either false or misunderstood:

> . . . and even if it did appear to come to him from God himself (like the command delivered to Abraham to slaughter his own son like a sheep) it is at least possible that in this instance a mistake has prevailed. [14]

Geoffrey Clive has found and translated a passage from Kant's collected works in which Kant went so far as to write what he thought Abraham should have replied to this voice which claimed to be the voice of God:

> That I ought not to kill my good son is certain beyond a shadow of a doubt; that you, as you appear to be, are God, I am not convinced and will never be even if your voice would resound from the [visible] heavens. [15]

At any rate, Kierkegaard thought that Abraham was a justified exception whose righteousness could not be explained in moral terms. And such an exception to moral rules proved, S.K. thought, that there must be a higher life, the religious life. Elsewhere I have argued that such justified exceptions can be accounted for within the area of ethics, and that, therefore, Kierkegaard's argument that they require us to postulate a higher life is a failure. [16] I still think that

is true, and perhaps philosophically important, but it may
also be beside the point here. Kierkegaard's main purpose
seems to have been not so much to prove that there is a
religious sphere—after all, we knew that some people led
religious lives, didn't we?—but to characterize that sphere,
to tell us what the authentic religious life is like.

How is the religious life different from the ethical?

First, and most obviously, again, Kierkegaard understood
the moral life to be a matter of universal rules; but Abraham
was a particular individual, and God's command came to
him alone: "Faith is precisely this paradox, that the
individual as the particular is higher than the universal, is
justified over against it, is not subordinated, but superior." [17]

This raises another question. If there *are* universal moral
rules, we should be able to know them and thus, in any given
case, prove to others that we are doing the right thing.
Kierkegaard thought this was possible. In our own day we
are plagued with ethical relativism, situation ethics, and
other such problems, and we may consider Kierkegaard's
(and Kant's) confidence rather naive. But, again, this may
be beside the point. The question is, how could Abraham
justify himself? How could he convince *anyone* that he was
doing the right thing? Remember that Abraham was a
hundred years old when Isaac was born. Suppose someone
saw Abraham taking his son up the mountain to the place
of sacrifice, carrying firewood and a knife, and figured out
what was happening! Suppose someone asked the old man
why he wanted to kill his son; what could Abraham say?
We could imagine the old man saying, "Well, I heard this
voice, you know, and it *said* it was the voice of God . . . it
did sound like God . . ." To put matters crudely, wouldn't
we think we were dealing with some kind of nut? At one

point in *Fear and Trembling*, Kierkegaard asks us to imagine that Isaac himself figured out what was happening. How could Abraham justify his action to his son? Perhaps he would not even try. Instead, something like the following might have happened:

> When Isaac again saw Abraham's face it was changed, his glance was wild, his form was horror. He seized Isaac by the throat, threw him to the ground, and said, "Stupid boy, dost thou then suppose that I am thy father? I am an idolater. Dost thou suppose that this is God's bidding? No, it is my desire!" Then Isaac trembled and cried out in his terror. "O God in heaven, have compassion upon me. If I have no father upon earth, be Thou my father!" But Abraham in a low voice said to himself, "O Lord in heaven, I thank Thee. After all it is better for him to believe that I am a monster, rather than that he should lose faith in Thee." [18]

This moving passage is intended to show us that Abraham couldn't justify himself to anyone, not even his own son. If he had tried, even his own son would have thought him a madman. Kierkegaard sometimes spoke of the religious man as a "knight of faith." In the following passage Kierkegaard effectively contrasts the relatively comfortable position of the moral man with the frightening situation of the religious man, the "knight of faith":

> He who believes that it is easy enough to be the individual can always be sure that he is not a knight of faith, for vagabonds and roving geniuses are not men of faith. The knight of faith knows, on the other hand, that it is glorious to belong to the universal. He knows that it is beautiful and salutary to be the individual who translates himself into the universal, to edit as it were, a pure and elegant edition of himself, as free from errors as possible and which everyone can read. He knows that it is refreshing to become intelligible to oneself in the universal so

that he understands it and so that every individual who understands him understands through him in turn the universal. He
knows that it is beautiful to be born as the individual who has
the universal as his home. . . . But he knows that higher than
this there winds a solitary path, narrow and steep; he knows
that it is terrible to be born outside the universal, to walk without
meeting a single traveller. He knows very well where he is and
how he is related to men. Humanly speaking, he is crazy and
cannot make himself intelligible to anyone.[19]

And what of Abraham himself, this "knight of faith" who
walked "a solitary path, narrow and steep"? How could he
be sure that he had heard the voice of God? Isn't it always
possible that alleged divine revelations are mistaken? The
great Jewish theologian and philosopher Martin Buber has
an essay entitled "The Suspension of Ethics" in which he
claims that this is *the* question.

"Where, therefore, the 'suspension' of the ethical conscience is concerned, the question of questions which takes
precedence over every other is: Are you really addressed by
the Absolute or by one of his apes?" [20]

Buber reminds us that we are today, as men have always
been, surrounded by false absolutes. Men claim to be
obeying the voice of God and yet do the most terrible things.
We need only remember the tortures of "infidels" in God's
holy name by the Spanish Inquisition and the Nazi killing
of six million Jews for the Third Reich. Even today bombs
continue to explode for the Revolution, or for Communism,
or to "kill the pigs," or to "keep those niggers in their place,"
and so on. No cause is *so* disreputable that it has not at some
time or other been defended by men who claimed to follow
the direct commands of God. How could Abraham have
known that he was right?

Kierkegaard does not answer this question. He rather uses
it for his own purposes. He might have replied, "Why do

you think I gave the book the title *Fear and Trembling?*"
Of course, Abraham couldn't have been completely sure; he
must have had his doubts. As Kierkegaard put it,

> The ethical expression for what Abraham did is, that he would
> murder Isaac; the religious expression is, that he would sacrifice
> Isaac; but precisely in this contradiction consists the dread which
> can well make a man sleepless, and yet Abraham is not what he
> is without this dread.[21]

Martin Luther may or may not have actually said, "Here
I stand, I cannot do otherwise," when he made the decision
that changed his own life and altered the course of religious
history. But Kierkegaard would have regarded this remark
as typical of the religious life. It is a mistake to think of the
religious man as some sort of rationalist with a new theory
which he seeks to defend, and for which he tries to win
adherents. Rather, the religious man witnesses to the truth
as he sees it. He cannot prove his case, but he risks everything for it. Abraham, like Luther, took his stand, and could
not do otherwise. If he had been wrong, he would have been
guilty of the murder of his only son. This is certainly ample
cause for fear and trembling.

IBSEN: KIERKEGAARD'S POET

Kierkegaard, as mentioned earlier, loved literature, music,
and the theater. He would have been pleased to see his work
illustrated in these media. Geoffrey Clive has written an
article in which he details several instances of Kierkegaardian thought in nineteenth-century literature.[22] Here I should
like to mention only the most outstanding, the work of the
great Norwegian playwright Henrik Ibsen (1828–1906).

Ibsen's writing has so many echoes of the work of

Kierkegaard that he is often called "Kierkegaard's poet."
It would be easy just to say that he was influenced by S.K.'s
work, and this is often claimed. But Ibsen himself denied
any such influence; artists always like to feel that their work
is original. We know, however, that Ibsen had read at least
part of *Either/Or* and *Fear and Trembling*. We know, too,
that Ibsen was in Copenhagen in 1852, nine years after
these works had been published. And his best friend,
Christopher Bruun, a young theology student, was an ardent
Kierkegaardian. Ibsen certainly heard a lot about Kierkegaard and may have been more influenced than he knew.
At any rate, Ibsen's work *does* convey much of the thought
of Kierkegaard, whether or not Ibsen intended it to.

By far the clearest expression of Kierkegaardian thought
in Ibsen's work is the long verse play *Brand* (1865). Brand,
a Lutheran minister, preaches a very strict doctrine, and
much of that doctrine is Kierkegaardian. Early in the play,
Brand calls upon Agnes (whom he later marries) to follow
him and to accept the life of duty that he must lead:

> Remember, I am stern in my demands. I require All or Nothing.
> No half measures. There is no forgiveness for failure. It may
> not be enough to offer your life. Your death may be needed
> also. . . . Choose. You stand at a parting of the ways.[23]

This certainly must remind the reader of Kierkegaard's
"either/or." It is obvious that Ibsen here emphasizes choice,
as Kierkegaard did. Also, the choice is absolute. Kierkegaard's
choice, "either/or" in the sense of *aut/aut*, amounts to nothing less than a demand for "all or nothing." This demand is
Brand's watchword and is repeated several times in the drama.

For Brand, as for Kierkegaard, importance is placed on
self-realization. Brand says: "A man must be himself. Only
thus can he carry his cause to victory." [24]

Brand also glorifies the individual, as did Kierkegaard. In the following passage the provost of the district in which Brand is serving as priest rebukes him for treating his parishioners as persons and urging them to be individuals:

> Your job isn't to save every Jack and Jill from damnation, but to see that the parish as a whole finds grace. We want all men to be equal. But you are creating inequality where it never existed before. Until now each man was simply a member of the Church. You have taught him to look upon himself as an individual, requiring special treatment. This will result in the most frightful confusion. The surest way to destroy a man is to turn him into an individual. Very few men can fight the world alone.[25]

Even more important than the above similarities is the fact that in *Brand* there is an instance of what Kierkegaard called a teleological suspension of ethical duties in favor of religious duties. Brand's parish is located near a frozen fjord in a valley that never sees the light of the sun. His young son becomes ill and Brand is told by the local doctor that if he does not take his son to a warmer climate, the boy will die. This would mean that Brand would have to leave his church. Thus, his ethical duty to love and care for his son is in conflict with his religious duty toward his church. Like Kierkegaard in *Fear and Trembling*, Ibsen most certainly had the story of Isaac and Abraham in mind, for when Agnes tries to comfort her husband with the thought that surely God would not let the boy die, Brand replies: "But if He should dare? If He should test me as He tested Abraham?"[26]

Brand chooses to fulfill his duty toward his church and the boy dies. Again, Brand chose his religious duty, though this action required that he ignore his ethical duty toward his son.

We should not suppose, however, that *Brand* or any other

work by Ibsen is absolutely Kierkegaardian. We can see at
least two major differences. First, Ibsen was simply not very
interested in religion. Whereas Kierkegaard sought to lead
us beyond the ethical to the religious, Ibsen's later works developed further (than S.K. had) the ethic of self-realization.
I think it could be argued that Ibsen went too far in
this direction. Thus in *A Doll's House* (1879), Nora leaves
her husband and family to go out and find herself. We get
the idea that there is an "ideal self" which Nora has lost
sight of, and which she must go out and find. In *Hedda
Gabler* (1890) we find a defense of suicide, based on the
ethic of self-realization. Hedda finds that she cannot be the
sort of wife that she should be, and, in danger of being
forced by the evil Judge Brack to become something that
she does not wish to be, she shoots herself. Again, suicide
is justified on grounds of self-realization.

A second difference between Kierkegaard's work and that
of Ibsen, especially *Brand,* is that for Kierkegaard's ethical
characters, the aesthetic is no longer the ruling principle,
although it is still present. There is pleasure in the ethical
life and in the religious life. (Remember the long section
of *Either/Or,* volume 2, entitled "The Aesthetic Validity of
Marriage" which was discussed earlier in this chapter.) And
despite the fact that the religious man suffers, he is also
happy, because, paradoxically, this very suffering here on
earth is his assurance of God's favor. Kierkegaard often said
that the three spheres—aesthetic, ethical, and religious—
should be regarded as "three great allies." This is not the
case in Ibsen's *Brand.* In this play the pleasures of the
aesthetic sphere are simply absent. Geoffrey Clive com-
mented on this in the article mentioned earlier:

For Brand there is no middle ground between holiness and nothingness. In creating him, Ibsen personified the Kierkegaardian 'Or' to the exclusion rather than the dethronement of the 'Either'.[27]

Let us return for a final word on Kierkegaard's *Fear and Trembling*. To grasp fully the import of Kierkegaard's treatment of the story of Abraham and Isaac, we need to remind ourselves once more of the cultural milieu against which S.K. was rebelling: Kant and then Hegel had expressed complete confidence in the power of reason to provide guidance in all questions, including questions of right and wrong. For Kant, especially, ethics was a completely rational matter, as borne out by the title of his book *Religion Within the Limits of Reason Alone*. As Kierkegaard saw it, the religion of his day, especially his own Danish Lutheran Church, had little need for fear and trembling; indeed, it closely paralleled the philosophy of his day. Religion, too, was held to be completely rational. Kierkegaard insisted that this was a mistake. But now an examination of his conception of the religious sphere is long overdue.

IV. The Religious Life:
Preliminary Considerations

When we say here in chapter 4 that *now* we're ready to discuss Kierkegaard's views on religion, the reader may well ask, "Haven't we been doing that all along?" And of course in one sense we certainly have, because Kierkegaard's whole effort was devoted to this matter of becoming a Christian. He was thus concerned with religion from the start. We are, then, emphasizing one aspect of S.K.'s thought, though the whole of that thought is directed toward religion.

S.K. AND THE DANISH LUTHERAN CHURCH

Kierkegaard was not primarily interested in writing to the non-Christian world. He wasn't trying to convert the heathen, so to speak. Thus if I were to say, "I'm a Zen Buddhist, and I've read Kierkegaard, and do not find in his writings any arguments that would lead me to change," this may be true, but it's also unfair criticism. This was never Kierkegaard's aim, so, again, it is hardly fair to say that he "failed" in it.

Unlike others who *did* write "contra Gentiles" (e.g., St. Thomas Aquinas), Kierkegaard presented no proofs for the existence of God in his writings. Philosophers generally agree that such "proofs" are inconclusive, anyway. But Kierkegaard was opposed to them for other reasons, only two of which need mention here. First, if the proofs *did* work, we could stop all this talk about *belief* in God, and about faith: "Anything that is almost probable, or probable, or extremely and emphatically probable, is something he can almost know, or as good as know, or extremely and emphatically almost *know*—but it is impossible to believe." [1] Take a simple example. I *know* that two plus two equals four. I don't *believe* this, or have *faith* that it is so; I know it. But the Christian religion is a religion of faith. Second, Kierkegaard points out that whenever we feel that we have to *prove* something, the whole matter becomes suspicious from the start:

> To defend anything is always to discredit it. Let a man have a storehouse full of gold, let him be willing to dispense every ducat to the poor—but let him besides that be stupid enough to begin this benevolent undertaking with a defense in which he advances three reasons to prove that it is justifiable—and people will be almost inclined to doubt whether he is doing any good. But now for Christianity! Yea, he who defends it has never believed it. [2]

Because of my own multiple insecurities I think of the writer who—as was once fashionable—begins his book with a lengthy defense of his having written it. He might begin, "Why, the reader may ask, do we need yet another book on Kierkegaard? Aren't there books enough on him, by major

scholars? Why another? Well, I have seventeen reasons for
writing. First . . ." Maybe the reader wasn't suspicious
before, but he will be now! S.K. obviously thinks multiple
proofs for the existence of God have the same effect.

Probably neither of these factors explains why S.K. has
no interest in proofs for the existence of God. Rather, it may
be that he was writing for those who were already convinced
of it. He wrote for those who were already Christians, after
a fashion, and what he hoped to do was get these "Christians"
to become true followers of Christ. S.K. often claimed that
nothing is more difficult than being a Christian in Christendom. Thus his description of the religious sphere is not an
attempt to convert non-Christians, but to tell those of us who
claim to be Christians what the Christian life is really like.

THE INFLUENCE OF FEUERBACH

Of course Kierkegaard was writing against the influence
of Hegel. But it is my opinion that the one single religious
author who most influenced Kierkegaard was a student of
Hegel, Ludwig Feuerbach (1804–1872), and that this influence is not sufficiently recognized. There are at least three
references to Feuerbach in Kierkegaard's work. In *Stages on
Life's Way* he notes that Feuerbach agrees with him that a
Christian's life is often characterized by suffering,
"Feuerbach, who pays homage to the principle of healthy-
mindedness says that the religious existence (more particularly the Christian) is a constant history of suffering." [3]
Elsewhere, Kierkegaard praises Feuerbach by referring to
him as "a scoffer [who] attacks Christianity and at the same
time expounds it so reliably that it is a pleasure to read him,
and one who is in perplexity about finding it distinctly set
forth may also have recourse to him." [4]

A third reference to Feuerbach is, I think, crucial for an understanding of Kierkegaard's religious thought:

> But that that which in accordance with its nature is eternal comes into existence in time, is born, grows up, and dies—this is a breach with all thinking. If on the other hand the becoming of the eternal in time is to be an eternal becoming—then ". . . all theology is anthropology," Christianity is transformed from an existence-communication into a metaphysical doctrine appropriate to professors. . . .[5]

The first statement of this passage presumably refers to Kierkegaard's account of the Incarnation as the "absolute paradox" of Christianity. But with what is this being contrasted? Understanding the contrast requires some understanding of Feuerbach's position.

The Essence of Christianity (1841), Feuerbach's most important work, is divided into two parts. In the first Feuerbach discusses the many mysteries of Christianity and explains these mysteries in psychological terms. The following quotation from a chapter entitled "The Mystery of the Resurrection" is a typical example:

> Man, at least in a state of ordinary well-being, has the wish not to die. This wish is originally identical with the instinct of self-preservation. Whatever lives seeks to maintain itself, to continue alive, and consequently not to die. Subsequently, when reflection and feeling are developed under the urgency of life, this primary negative wish becomes the positive wish for a life, and that a better life, after death. But this wish involves the further wish for a certainty of its fulfilment. Reason can afford no such certainty. It has therefore been said that all proofs of immortality are insufficient and even that unassisted reason is not capable of apprehending it, still less of proving it. And with justice; for reason furnishes only general proofs; it cannot give the certainty of any personal immortality, and it is precisely this certainty that is desired. Such a certainty requires an immediate

personal assurance, a practical demonstration. This can only be
given to me by the fact of a dead person, whose death has been
previously certified, rising again from the grave; and he must
be no indifferent person, but, on the contrary, the type and
representative of all others, so that his resurrection also may be
the type, the guarantee of theirs. The resurrection of Christ is
therefore the satisfied desire of man for an immediate certainty
of his personal existence after death. . . .[6]

The point here is that we believe in the risen Christ and
in our own resurrection because of our wish to be immortal.
The mystery is, then, explained in terms of the wish. If this
language of "wish-fulfillment"—and, indeed, this entire
discussion—sound familiar and almost commonplace, this is
a tribute to Feuerbach's genius. He anticipated much of the
modern psychological thought regarding religious truths.
Two points must be emphasized here. The mystery is
explained in terms of a wish, and the wish is *man's* wish. If
this is granted (and of course I am not for a moment suggesting that we grant it), it follows that to understand
religion is not to understand God, but to understand *man*,
for we create our notion of God from our ideals, hopes, and
wishes. In other words, man created God in his own image
—not, though, as man was, but as he wanted to be.

From this account of what he took to be the truth about
Christianity Feuerbach moves in the second part of the book
to a criticism of the beliefs of orthodox Christianity, e.g.,
the belief in the literal truth of such mysteries as the resurrection. Feuerbach considered orthodox Christianity an
unacceptable alternative to the reasoned explanation he had
given in the first part of his book. He tried to explain this
by demonstrating that the orthodox view of Christianity is
full of contradictions. Part 2 of *The Essence of Christianity*
is entirely devoted to the tasks of pointing out the contra-

dictions in Christian doctrines. In part 2 Feuerbach devotes a chapter to "The Contradiction of the Nature of God in General" from which the following is taken:

> The fundamental idea [of God] is a contradiction which can be concealed only by sophisms. A God who does not trouble himself about us, who does not hear our prayers, who does not see us and love us, is no God;—but at the same time it is said: a God who does not exist in and by himself, out of men, above men, as another being, is a phantom; and thus it is made an essential predicate of God that he is non-human and extra-human. A God who is not as we are, who has not consciousness, not intelligence, i.e., not a personal understanding, a personal consciousness . . . is no God. Essential identity with us is the chief condition of deity, the idea of deity is made dependent on the idea of personality, of consciousness. . . . But it is said in the same breath, a God who is not essentially distinguished from us is no God.[7]

Without going too far into theology, let us pause here to emphasize the fact that this really is a problem which must be faced by anyone who tries to think seriously about the Christian doctrine. Let me mention two examples.

The first example is taken from the early work of the great British poet, John Milton (1608–1674), the author of *Paradise Lost*, considered by many the greatest poem in the English language. As a young man he wrote several short poems on various events in the life of Christ. "On the Morning of Christ's Nativity," written in 1629, described the coming of Christ into our world as like the coming of "the mighty Pan," and said of him in stanza 25, "Our Babe to show his Godhead true,/Can in his swadling bands control the damned crew."

"The Passion," an undated poem, must have been written at about the same time. In it Milton speaks in these terms of

Christ taking a human form: "O what a Mask was there, what a disguise."

As the poem goes on, Milton writes about the suffering of Christ on the Cross, his death, and other events of the Passion. The tears flow, but somehow the whole thing fails to "come off." The tears get bigger, as Milton reminds us of the agony of Jesus, but somehow the poem is unconvincing. Then it just stops. Milton appended a note which read, "This Subject the Author finding to be above the years he had, when he wrote it, and nothing satisfied with what was begun, left it unfinisht." [8]

Why was the poem left "unfinisht"? Perhaps it was because Milton could not reconcile the attributes of Christ. If the birth of Christ, his taking of a human form, was a "mask" and a "disguise," then wasn't his death—and his pain on the cruel cross—a fake too? Milton made Christ God at the cost of letting him be human. But, really now, can we believe that he could actually be "very God" who "was made man," as the creed says? Is this possible? Feuerbach thought it was not.

Take another example. While I was a graduate student, a noted British theologian came to our campus and spoke to a philosophy class of which I was a member. One of my fellow students was bold enough to ask the theologian if he believed in the virgin birth. After a moment of hesitation, the theologian replied, "Yes, but I wish I didn't." The theologian explained by saying that he had once been a prison chaplain and that one day when visiting a hardened criminal in a Liverpool jail he had sought to convict him of his sinful condition by saying, "Don't you sometimes feel terribly guilty when you compare your sinful life with that of our example, the completely pure and sinless life of Jesus

Christ?" The criminal sat quietly for a long moment, and then objected, "Aye, but he didn't start fair." The point should be obvious; Jesus was God, so of course he would be free from human sin, but what relevance has this fact for you or me? Again, I am not trying to do theology here, but to emphasize the fact that it is easy to argue that the Christian faith *seems* to have contradictions in it. And this is one of them: can we reconcile the fact that Jesus Christ was God with the apparently conflicting fact that he was also human, "very God" who "was made man"?

So much for examples. Let us return to Feuerbach, who, in his Preface, summed up what he thought he had accomplished in his book:

> I find therein the *truth*, the *essence* of religion, that it conceives and affirms a profoundly human relation as a divine relation; on the other hand, in the second part I show that the son of God (in Theology) . . . is not a son in the natural, human sense, but in an entirely different manner, contradictory to Nature and reason, and therefore absurd, and I find in this negation of human sense and the human understanding, the negation of religion. Accordingly the first part is the *direct*, the second the *indirect* proof, that theology is anthropology.[9]

The reader should note that Feuerbach uses "anthropology" *very* generally to include *all* the studies in which man is the object of study, for example, anthropology in the usual sense, history, psychology, and so on.

If we look closely at the last quotation from Kierkegaard concerning Feuerbach, we can see that Feuerbach's work seems to have confronted Kierkegaard with an "either/or." *Either* the reader accepts Feuerbach's reasoned (principally psychological) explanation of the mysteries of Christianity or he must accept the fact that Christianity seems to be full

of contradictions. I shall argue that Kierkegaard did not
think of Christian doctrine as *really* full of contradictions,
though Christianity *is* paradoxical on his view, that is, it is
full of what seem to be contradictions. He certainly wanted
to reject any account of Christianity such as that propounded
by Feuerbach which would give a completely reasoned
account of religion.

I think we can see the influence of Feuerbach in the fact
that Kierkegaard spoke of two types of religious life, which
he sometimes spoke of as "Religiousness 'A' " and "Religiousness 'B'." Again, these can be better understood with
examples.

THE RELIGION OF ABSOLUTE PARADOX

Consider this example. Suppose I own an acre of land in
Texas. I somehow come to believe that there is oil on my
land. I sell all I have (house, car, personal belongings, etc.)
and invest in drilling equipment. I borrow all the money
I can to drill the well deeper. I risk financial ruin for the
sake of that oil well. Now, if you saw me giving everything
for the sake of that well, wouldn't you think, "Surely he
knows something we don't; surely he knows that there is oil
beneath his land." But suppose I didn't; suppose I couldn't
prove that there was oil beneath my land. Wouldn't my
action be paradoxical?

Let me define that term *paradoxical*. A paradox is a
seeming contradiction, and the paradox is said to be resolved
when we show that the contradiction is only apparent. In the
case of my drilling for a well, my action seems to contradict
(in an admittedly extended sense of *contradict*) my lack of
knowledge. This would suffice as an example of Religious-

ness "A." The case of Abraham would also suffice as an example. He could not prove that he had heard the voice of God, but he believed, and risked his only son for his belief. Notice, before we leave my example, that there *could* be oil on my land; I simply don't know, and can't prove that there is. Similarly, if there is a God, Abraham could have heard his voice; he simply could not prove that he had. The "paradox" of Religiousness "A" is that the believer acts, and risks so much, on less than complete knowledge.

There is another aspect of Abraham's case that I have deliberately neglected until now. The Bible says that "Abraham believed God," but what, exactly, was it that he believed? Well, he believed that God had given him a *promise:* that in their old age, Abraham and his wife Sarah would have a son, Isaac, and that through Isaac, Abraham would be the father of a great nation. But then later God came to Abraham with a *command:* that he should take Isaac to the place of sacrifice and kill him. Now the problem should be clear; how could Abraham believe both the promise and the command? The two, taken together, would seem to make no sense. If Abraham was to sacrifice Isaac, then Isaac could produce no grandsons for him. Or, if Isaac was to make Abraham the father of a great nation, then Isaac was not to be sacrificed. In an excellent article on this topic, Professor Robert Herbert raises the question of whether or not Kierkegaard thought of Abraham's case as involving a logical contradiction:

> One might wish to say so. For if the promise is that through Isaac Abraham's seed should be multiplied as the stars of heaven and the command is that Isaac should be sacrificed, then the promise and the command in conjunction involve that a dead boy should grow to manhood, marry, and father children . . . we

might wish to say 'A dead boy cannot grow up, marry, and father children', in order to point out that . . . the promise and the command in conjunction make no sense.[10]

But Professor Herbert has also discovered a passage in Kierkegaard's *Fear and Trembling* which proved that Abraham was never asked to believe a self-contradiction:

> Let us go further. We let Isaac be really sacrificed. Abraham believed. He did not believe that some day he would be blessed in the beyond, but that he would be happy here in the world. God . . . would recall him who had been sacrificed.[11]

Commenting on this passage, Herbert writes:

> This shows that Kierkegaard did not regard Abraham as one who was being asked to 'believe' the logically impossible, or the nonsensical, whatever it might mean to say of one that he believes such. There is rather, something that we should call fulfillment of the promise, even though the command had been obeyed.[12]

Herbert has shown how the paradox in the case of Abraham and Isaac could be resolved. It is Herbert's belief that there are no contradictions or logical impossibilities in Kierkegaard's entire account of the religious sphere, but he does not claim to have proved this conclusively.

We must be sure that we are being clear and not racing ahead of the account. At least two ideas here need to be talked about further. First, Kierkegaard distinguishes Religiousness "A" and "B" in the following way: In "A," the believer makes his choice, risks all for it, though he cannot prove the truth of that for which he risks everything. S.K. thought that all religion is like that, paradoxical in that sense. One could imagine a simple deism, just the belief that some sort of creator God must exist, though we cannot know his nature. This would be an example of Religiousness "A." In the case of Religiousness "B," however, we have a double paradox, so to speak (using Kierkegaard's terminology). Not only is it impossible (as in Religiousness "A") for the believer to prove his case, to prove that God exists, for example, but *what* he is expected to believe is also paradoxical. We have, I hope, already seen this in the case of Abraham and Isaac. But the most obvious case of Religiousness "B" is the Christian faith. We are not only asked to believe that Jesus Christ once walked the earth (and this we can't prove) but we are also expected to believe he was at once human and divine, that he was a historical personage and yet eternal. So we are expected to believe what appear to be contradictions concerning this central figure of our faith:

> The historical fact [that is, that when Jesus was born a God-man came into being] which is the content of our hypothesis has a peculiar character, since it is not an ordinary historical fact, but a fact based on a self-contradiction.[13]

A favorite problem for Kierkegaard scholars is that of deciding whether Kierkegaard thought of Christianity as involving genuine contradictions or only *seeming* contradictions which we could resolve, given greater knowledge. Kierkegaard is sometimes thought of as a complete irrationalist, one who asked us to accept a faith that is paradoxical and absurd. The problem is, of course, compounded by the fact that he often uses these very words, *absurd* and *paradoxical,* in reference to Christianity. I think it is possible to show, by a careful examination of Kierkegaard's texts and secondary sources, that Kierkegaard never intended that the Christian should be one who believed a self-contradiction.[14]

Again, we need to remind ourselves that Kierkegaard always wrote with a definite audience in mind. If we forget this we are in the position of someone examining a set of answers without knowing what questions have been asked. He was addressing an audience that thought of Christianity as a completely rational doctrine, which could be fully understood, proved true once and for all. S.K. thought that the Danish Lutherans didn't *do* anything about it, but they certainly had the doctrine worked out.

CHRISTIANITY AND "SUBJECTIVE TRUTH"

Up to now, in my exposition of the religious sphere, Kierkegaard has argued that even considered as a doctrine, Christianity has been misunderstood. We cannot prove the existence of God, and the doctrine at least *seems* to be shot through with logical contradictions. Whether or not genuine contradictions are involved is another matter, a subject that has evoked considerable discussion. But we can safely assert (and perhaps this is all that Kierkegaard would have wanted) that, considered simply as a doctrine, Christianity is . . . well, as one wag put it, "This simple doctrine is not as simple as many simple people believe."

But should the Christian religion be considered a doctrine at all? Kierkegaard's major work on the religious life bears the title *Concluding Unscientific Postscript*. The title bears closer examination. What does he mean by "unscientific"? Walter Lowrie tells us that the Danish word *uvidenskabelig* has a wider application than our word.[15] The German word *wissenschaftlich* is often translated as scientific, and so is the Danish term, though the German is related to *wissen* ("to know") and is thus much wider in application than *scientific*.

The point seems to be nothing less than that we are not primarily concerned with knowledge at all. One way of putting the case would be to say that Kierkegaard means to appeal not to the intellect but to the will. Again, he thought people knew (or thought they knew) enough about Christian doctrine; now it is time to actually *become* Christians.

A related point made by Kierkegaard has caused a lot of confusion. Chapter 2 of part 2 of *Concluding Unscientific Postscript* is entitled, "The Subjective Truth, Inwardness; Truth is Subjectivity." What could it mean to speak of truth as "subjective"? Let me mention one possible answer. Suppose I hold up a flower and ask a group, "What color is the flower?" Most of the class replies, "Red." But one person says, "Yellow." Usually we would say that the flower has just the color it has (that's an objective fact) and we are agreed that it's red; the maverick who says it's yellow is either lying or has defective vision. *But* someone might say, "Well, each person sees things as they appear to him. So the flower is red *to us*. But if he says it's yellow, then it's yellow. It's yellow *to him*; truth is a subjective matter." I shall not even attempt a reply to this sort of skepticism, but only say that this is *not* what Kierkegaard means. And this is worth saying, because he has been so interpreted. But let us turn to what Kierkegaard himself had to say. First, consider a puzzling passage:

> When the question of truth is raised in an objective manner, reflection is directed objectively to the truth, as an object to which the knower is related. If only the object to which he is related is the truth, the subject is accounted to be in the truth. When the question of the truth is raised subjectively, reflection is directed subjectively to the nature of the individual's relationship; if only the mode of this relationship is in the truth, the

individual is in the truth, even if he should happen to be thus
related to what is not true.[16]

This notion of "subjective truth" can be difficult to understand. Subjective truth is not a truth that one *knows*, in the
sense that we can know that the statement "The flower is
red" is true. This would be an example of "objective truth."
Kierkegaard apparently calls "subjective truth" *subjective*
because the notion refers to the individual (i.e., the subject).
It is the individual's *relationship* that counts when we speak
of "subjective truth."

In one of Kierkegaard's examples, he asks that we imagine
two men going to places of worship to pray. One of these
men is a Christian, the other a pagan. But the Christian
merely praises himself and asks for favors while the pagan
prays with fervor, prostrates himself, and fully commits himself to his beliefs. The question is: where is there more truth?
And Kierkegaard's answer is, "The one prays in truth to
God though he worships an idol; the other prays falsely to
the true God, and hence worships in truth an idol." [17] That
should do it. What counts in the religious life is "subjective
truth," and this refers to the believer's relationship. The
pagan worshiped in the right way; he led a religious life.
The "Christian" was not religious, not really. We could say
that this "Christian" was not really "in the truth," and when
we talk that way, we mean what Kierkegaard called "subjective truth."

Kierkegaard wanted us to become Christians. But, we
may ask, how exactly do we become Christians? And why
should we? What is so attractive about the Christian faith?

Kierkegaard has been criticized for his answer to the
first question. He said that we become Christians, that we

move into the religious sphere from the ethical, by a "leap of faith." As he put it, "Reflection can be halted only by a leap. . . . When the subject does not put an end to his reflection, he is made infinite in reflection, i.e., he does not arrive at a decision." [18]

This may sound mad, but consider examples. A young man asks the girl he loves to marry him. She needs time to consider an answer. She wants to be convinced that he is the "right" man before she can decide. So she talks to his mother and father to learn what he is like at home. She talks to his younger brothers and sisters to see how good he is with children. She talks to his minister, his teachers, his psychiatrist (if any). But now we're getting a bit silly, aren't we? If a girl must wait until *all* the facts are in, until all the information relevant to a good marriage has been collected, she will never decide. She will never marry this boy or any other.

The case is the same with Christianity. It is not my business to dwell on such old evangelical hymns as "Almost Persuaded." But the message is the same. Whether we are deciding to become Christians, or to get married, or anything else, we finally must put reflection aside, and make our decision. S.K. has been criticized for this, by, among others, his fellow Dane, Harald Höffding: "To pronounce this concept of a leap valid is purely arbitrary." [19] Here I think Kierkegaard can be defended. He did not say that reasons cannot be given for a choice. The young girl asks for reasons, and should have them, before she decides to marry. But, in the very nature of the case, she can never know *all* the facts. She must decide on less than complete evidence, and so must the Christian. If we wait for complete knowledge, we shall never decide.

Here Kierkegaard was reacting once more against Hegel
and the Hegelian notion that when the system is complete,
we can know everything. And he may have overreacted. But
S.K. is surely right that the tragedy of a man who is "almost
persuaded"—about anything—is that if he waits for complete knowledge he can never decide, for he waits for what
he can never have.

But what sort of reasons are there for becoming a Christian? We have shown that Kierkegaard thought that the doctrine could not be proved, that indeed it was paradoxical.
Maybe the best reason for becoming a Christian is that a
Christian will be blessed of God and can have everything he
wants here and now (prosperity, wealth, health, happiness,
and so on) and the fringe benefit of eternal bliss in heaven.
No, Kierkegaard thought that the Christian must suffer here
on earth. The heads of the Church in Denmark (Mynster,
Martensen, and others) did not, and this was one of the main
reasons Kierkegaard thought they were not really "witnesses
to the truth." Ibsen conveyed Kierkegaard's beliefs on the
subject in his play *Brand*, I think, although the words are
not really Kierkegaard's. In a scene late in the play, the
minister, Brand, is leading a group of his parishioners up
the mountain to build a new church, to expand God's work.
They begin to question him:

> Schoolmaster: There's no question of our lives being
> endangered?
> A Man: What will be my share of the reward?
> A Woman: My son will not die, will he, Father?
> Sexton: Will victory be ours by Tuesday?
> Brand [*stares at them, bewildered*]: What are you asking?
> What do you want to know?
> Sexton: First, how long will we have to fight? Secondly, how
> much will it cost us? Thirdly, what will be our reward?

Brand: That is what you want to know?
Schoolmaster: Yes; you didn't tell us.
Brand [*angrily*]: Then I shall tell you now.
Crowd: Speak! Speak!
Brand: How long will you have to fight? Until you die! What will it cost? Everything you hold dear. Your reward? A new will, cleansed and strong, a new faith, integrity of spirit; a crown of thorns. That will be your reward.
Crowd [*screams in fury*]: Betrayed! You have betrayed us! You have tricked us! [20]

Then the crowd leaves Brand. Perhaps it is always so. Didn't Jesus say something about the way being narrow, and didn't he suggest that this way would not be taken by many? In place of the easy intellectual faith of his day, Kierkegaard pointed to a more difficult path, a way of suffering.

This more difficult way can also be illustrated by other examples. One way we have of making Christianity a bit easier to swallow is by saying that Jesus and the Apostles didn't *really* mean what they said. In the *Journals*, S.K. wrote: "Most people really believe that the Christian commandments (e.g., to love one's neighbour as oneself) are intentionally a little severe—like putting the clock on half an hour to make sure of not being late in the morning." [21] Thus, we rule out adultery *except* when we love the girl, and we don't steal *unless* we really need the money. And obviously Jews and Negroes do not count as neighbors. But Kierkegaard took the example of Christ seriously.

And what about this example of Christ? Is this an attractive example? Do we really want to be as he was? Kierkegaard insisted that we don't. "Just try to imagine quite clearly to yourself that the model is called a 'Lamb'; that alone is a scandal to natural man, no one has any desire to be a lamb." [22]

So the model is not attractive. We follow a Jewish car-
penter who was born in a stable and grew up to die as a
sacrificial lamb. Is that really what we want to do with *our*
lives?

One example that suggests itself is the story (which may
or may not be true) of a noted preacher who once gave a
special sermon at a university chapel service. The subject
was missionary work, and the speaker waxed eloquent. "Who
will go?" he asked. "Who will take the message of Christ
to the steaming, disease-ridden jungles of Africa? Who will
seek out the black savages who have never heard the story
of the Savior; who will go to save those dying in heathen
darkness?" The speaker paused for emphasis, and the silence
was broken by a young girl who was sitting on the first row,
"I'll go," she said softly; "I'll go, father." It was the
preacher's own daughter, his only child! The preacher was
so shocked that he blurted out, "Oh *no!* Not you!" But—or
so the story has it—the young girl insisted that she *would*
go to the mission field, and go she did.

Why did Kierkegaard paint such a picture of Christian
faith—paradoxical, a life of suffering, shame, etc.? Of
course, he was replying to Hegel and Feuerbach and the
Danish Lutherans. But he also meant to be honest, to "tell
it like it is." And I find that young people respect his honesty;
they find S.K.'s difficult Christian faith—and the challenge
it involves—more appealing than some popular alternatives
that I shall not mention by name. But we might just whisper,
"Are *our* churches so different from those Kierkegaard criticized?" Surely his corrective is needed today, and his work
has been influential.

V. The Religious Life:
The Major Texts

A curious pedagogical technique I sometimes employ in my classes is first to lay out an outline of a philosopher's thought, and then, in subsequent lectures, go over the more obscure details in a somewhat more technical way. After the general overview in the last chapter of Kierkegaard's thought concerning the religious sphere of existence, here in chapter 5 a closer examination is attempted. It focuses on his two major works on the subject, the *Philosophical Fragments* and the *Concluding Unscientific Postscript*.

PLATO AND CHRISTIANITY

In his *Philosophical Fragments*, Kierkegaard draws a contrast between the philosophy of Plato (427–347 B.C.) and Christianity. Kierkegaard begins by asking, "How far does

the truth admit of being learned? With this question let us
begin. It was a Socratic question. . . ." [1]

Let *us* begin with the reminder that Socrates (469–399
B.C.) was the teacher of Plato. Socrates himself wrote nothing (among academicians there is a bad joke that he was
put to death because he didn't publish). At any rate, what
we know of Socrates we know largely through the *Dialogues*
of Plato, in which Socrates usually appears as the central
figure. We should admit at the outset that this causes problems. For one thing, how do we know that Socrates really
said all those things Plato attributed to him? Some philosophers think it possible to distinguish the writings of the
early Plato—in which, presumably, the historical Socrates
really did say them—from the "middle" dialogues and the
"later" dialogues, in which Socrates is used as the "mouth-
piece" for Plato's own thought. I remain unconvinced that
such nice distinctions can be made, and will, without preju-
dice, speak now of Plato's views and then of Socrates'
thought, as if the two were the same.

To return to the quotation, "How far does the truth admit
of being learned? . . . a Socratic question . . .": This suggests that S.K. is considering questions of epistemology, that
is, the theory of knowledge. Accordingly, a brief discussion
of Plato's theory of knowledge is in order.

Plato was basically a mathematician who took plane
geometry as a paradigm case of knowledge. Suppose, then,
a geometry teacher is giving a lecture on triangles. He draws
a few crude figures on the blackboard, talks about them.
After about fifty minutes, the bell rings and the students
leave. The teacher erases the board. Plato thought students
might learn a great deal in such classes. But what did they
learn, or what was their knowledge, knowledge of? Notice

that it is not the case that their knowledge is simply of the figures the teacher puts on the board, or else when the teacher erased the board he would have wiped away the objects of their knowledge. Suppose, further, that the geometry teacher were to point to one of the figures he had drawn and then ask the students, "Is this really (really) a triangle?" If the students were alert, they would reply that it was not. For triangles, according to Euclid's definitions, have sides that are line segments, having only position and direction, and no thickness. Obviously, we cannot draw figures with sides that have no thickness. So, as odd as it may sound, we could say there are no real triangles in the physical world. But Plato would have thought it more significant that our knowledge is not actually of figures drawn on any board. If the geometry students learn anything at all, they learn something about the very nature of triangularity itself. The important point is that they do not learn just about this or that triangle, but the universal truth about triangles, the very essence of triangles, what it is that makes a triangle a triangle.

And so it is with everything. Plato thought that our knowledge is always of universal truths. In the study of biology, for example, human anatomy, we seek a universal truth about the human body. In classes in political theory, we seek to know, not about this or that state, but about what makes a state a state, the very essence of the political unit. Again, a problem is that the world in which we live has only particulars, individual humans, and the states in which they live; we do not find any universals in *this* world.

Plato gave several bold answers to these puzzles. He said that since we know universal truths, they must exist, somewhere. So he postulated a world of universals, called the world of forms or ideas. These are the patterns, or sometimes the paradigms, for the individual things of earth. These must exist, he claimed, since our knowledge is knowledge of them. But how could we know them, if they do not exist in the present world? His response was that we, each of us, must have lived before, and in this previous existence, we knew the forms, these universal truths, directly.

This is not the place to quarrel with this philosophy. But there are relevant implications to be sorted out. Plato's view was that we all lived in some previous life in which, somehow, we knew the universals. In the present life we "learn" about them by being led to remember. In Plato's *Republic*, a group of young men and the aging Socrates set out to learn the nature of justice and of the ideal state. None of them are political science majors, and Socrates claims that he knows nothing. But they learn a great deal. How is this possible? Plato's answer is that, in *teaching* them, Socrates in fact only drew out what each already knew. He did this by asking leading questions, and then carefully examining each proposed answer, prodding the students to remember more and more.

Plato's epistemology is called the theory of recollection, for obvious reasons. Socrates led his pupils to "recollect" these truths about justice, virtue, the state, and so on. This theory explains the use of the dialogue form in Plato's writings, and also how Socrates could be a great teacher while claiming to know nothing; the "Socratic method of teaching" consisted merely of asking leading questions. One implication of this position is that the teacher who brings us to a knowledge of the truth can be just anybody, a person of no special qualifications whatever, because he doesn't tell us anything we didn't already know. Again, the teacher is really of little or no importance.[2]

One more point: suppose someone were to ask, "When did triangularity begin?" The question makes no sense, does it? Plato would have said the forms (in this case, triangularity) are eternal. We might not want to accept that, but these universals, whatever they are, are not historical, are they? Triangularity did not begin on a certain date; the forms do have a certain timelessness. Concerning all of this Kierkegaard said, "From the standpoint of the Socratic thought every point of departure in time is *eo ipso* accidental, an occasion, a vanishing moment. The teacher himself is no more than this. . . ." [3]

At this point, S.K. asks the reader to join him in what he calls a "project of thought." Let us see if we can imagine that things just might be otherwise than as Socrates has described them. In particular, let us suppose that, rather than being a mere occasion for learning, the moment is to be decisive in its significance, Kierkegaard's argument continues:

> This was Socrates' explanation [i.e. the doctrine of Recollection, described above]; we have seen what follows from it with respect to the moment. Now if the latter is to have decisive significance, the seeker must be destitute of the Truth up to the very moment of his learning it; he cannot even have possessed it in the form of ignorance, for in that case the moment becomes merely occasional.[4]

This may be puzzling because this expression "possessed it in the form of ignorance" is unfamiliar. We can only suppose that this refers to the Socratic (or Platonic) idea that, in one sense, one has always possessed the truth, since everyone has preexisted and known the forms directly; but at the same time one can be ignorant in the sense that he has "forgotten" these forms and needs to be reminded of them.

If we think of ourselves as being truly ignorant, as actually not knowing and not merely as standing in need of a
reminder, a difference in the role of the teacher occurs. The
teacher can no longer be one who merely asks leading questions; the teacher cannot be ignorant:

> Now if the learner is to acquire the Truth, the Teacher must
> bring it to him; and not only so, but he must also give him the
> condition for understanding it. For if the learner were in his
> own person the condition for understanding the Truth, he need
> only recall it.[5]

Here we must be on our guard because a good deal hangs
on this passage. It seems logical to assume that if a person
is without the truth, it must be brought to him. But is it
therefore true, in any ordinary sense, that the teacher must
also give the student the *condition* for learning? Surely it
is not true, for example, that in order to teach a child anything, the teacher must first give the child the mentality to
understand and accept this teaching. S.K. defends this du-
bious statement with a lot of verbal sleight of hand: "The
condition for understanding the Truth is like the capacity to
inquire for it: the condition contains the conditioned and the
question implies the answer." [6] Insofar as this means, literally, that in order to ask questions I must already know the
answers, the statement is clearly false.

The next paragraph of the *Fragments* shows how much
hangs on the passage quoted above:

> But one who gives the learner not only the Truth but also the
> condition for understanding it, is more than teacher. All in-
> struction depends upon the presence, in the last analysis, of the
> requisite condition; if this is lacking, no teacher can do anything.
> For otherwise he would find it necessary, not only to transform
> the learner, but to re-create him before beginning to teach him.

> But this is something that no human being can do; if it is to be done, it must be done by God himself . . . who in acting as on occasion prompts the learner to recall that he is in error, and that by reason of his own guilt. But this state, this being in Error by reason of one's own guilt, what shall we call it? Let us call it *Sin*.[7]

So the assertion that the learner, if he does not already know (as he does, according to the doctrine of recollection), must not only be given the Truth but also the conditions for learning it, has led to the conclusion that God must be the teacher—and "Error" is Sin. The passage quoted just above has caused confusion among Kierkegaard's readers. Marjorie Grene, for instance, objects to the passage and points to "the theological question of defining sin on this purely intellectual basis." [8] This conception of sin has little or nothing to do with the intellect. Sin is untruth, or Error, but the opposite of this, i.e., Truth, is not intellectual at all. The confusion in this passage is a result of the fact that Kierkegaard has here introduced his own special meaning for the word *Truth*. But this requires clarification.

Some of this clarification has already been given in the previous chapter, for Kierkegaard here means by Truth not the "objective" truth of propositions, but "subjective" truth. And this has to do not with *what* a person knows, but *how* he is related to what is known. Remember the example of the "Christian" who is a master of doctrine, who has taken several theology courses, who can quote Scripture at length, etc.—*but* (and this is decisive) really cares very little about his religion. On the other hand, a pagan is said to be "in the Truth" because his faith is the center of his whole existence; he truly loves his "false" god with all his heart, all his soul, all of what S.K. calls his "passionate inwardness."

Now the contrast is complete. On the one hand, in Plato's

system we are concerned with speculative truth. This truth is
objective and eternal. On the other hand, the time in which
we gain the truth is unimportant, since it is only an occasion
for recollection. And the teacher is of no consequence, since
he does not tell the learner anything he doesn't know, but
only prods his memory—and almost anyone can do that.
In the Christian faith, all this is different; everything is
changed. The Truth with which we are concerned is subjective, for we are concerned, not with the truth of propositions, but with our relation to God. The *time* in which Christ
appeared in history is so important that his appearing divided
all of history into before and after. And the *Teacher* is of
supreme importance; he is God incarnate in human form,
who, in bringing the Truth to the learner, performs nothing
less than a new act of creation! Kierkegaard is at his best
as he describes this "Project of Thought," and we know that
he is mocking the Danish Lutheran Church, as he pretends to
be coining new terms:

> What now shall we call such a Teacher, one who restores the
> lost condition and gives the learner the Truth? Let us call him
> *Saviour,* for he saves the learner from his bondage and from
> himself; let us call him *Redeemer,* for he redeems the learner
> from the captivity into which he had plunged himself, and no
> captivity is so terrible and so impossible to break, as that in
> which the individual keeps himself. And still we have not said
> all that is necessary; for by his self-imposed bondage the learner
> has brought upon himself burden of guilt, and when the Teacher
> gives him the condition and the Truth he constitutes himself an
> *Atonement,* taking away the wrath impending upon that of which
> the learner has made himself guilty.[9]

Not much has been written on this aspect of Kierkegaard's
thought, but S.K. seems to go even farther than Calvin, or
at least as far. Note that the "learner" does not simply de-

cide, of his own free will, to change; God must give him "the condition," that is, God must change the learner to make it possible for him to make the right choice. Not only did Kierkegaard believe the acceptance of the Christian faith requires a "leap"; God must first make this leap possible by re-creating the learner in the requisite sense. Again, S.K. describes this change as if he were coining a new term:

> In consequence of receiving the condition in the moment the course of his life has been given an opposite direction, so that he is now turned about. Let us call this change *Conversion*, even though this word be one not hitherto used; but that is precisely a reason for choosing it, in order namely to avoid confusion, for it is as if expressly coined for the change we have in mind.[10]

How often has the Christian faith been so beautifully set forth? The contrast is made, and explained in detail. Kierkegaard is intrigued by the fact that Christianity places such an emphasis on history. It is concerned with the eternal, and yet the historical remains a central feature. Thus near the end of the *Fragments* (a small book, which just stops rather abruptly) S.K. wrote:

> It is well known that Christianity is the only historical phenomenon which in spite of the historical, nay precisely by means of the historical, has offered itself to the individual as a point of departure for his eternal consciousness, has assumed to interest him in another sense than the merely historical, has proposed to base his eternal happiness on his relationship to something historical.[11]

WAS THE *POSTSCRIPT* A JOKE?

The full title of Kierkegaard's major theological work is *Concluding Unscientific Postscript to the Philosophical Fragments*. That much is known, but almost everything else in

the work is debatable. It is a large book. There is a touch
of humor involved in the fact that the *Postscript* is 544 pages
long, in the English translation, plus an appendix and notes,
compared to only 93 for the *Fragments*. (Have you ever
written a letter, and then added a "postscript" about five and
a half times as long as the letter?) The problem that leads
to the *Postscript* is that given in the last quote above, from
the *Fragments*.[12] The problem might be put this way: granted
that Christianity is in some sense historical; can it be understood (can I understand it?) in a way that makes it appropriate for a person to base his hopes for an eternal happiness
upon this understanding? Kierkegaard himself tells us that
this is the point of departure for the *Postscript*. So perhaps
we can agree on that much. S.K.'s commentators are agreed
on little else so far as this book is concerned. Some claim
that it is a masterwork of theology, others maintain that it
isn't theology at all; others say it is a major work in the
philosophy of existence, still others that it isn't philosophy
at all. At least one writer maintains that it's all a joke. In
what follows, I shall argue that there is a sense in which
the *Postscript* isn't *theology* at all (or philosophy either),
and really is what could (with qualifications) be called an
elaborate joke.

In a recent article, "Christianity and Nonsense," Henry E.
Allison notes that Kierkegaard, here once again, was poking
fun at the philosophy of Hegel, in an incredibly complicated
way. Allison maintains that S.K. had in mind, most especially, the defense of intellectual objectivity found in the
Phenomenology of Mind:

> The tendency towards objective thought finds its culmination
> in Hegel. In the Hegelian philosophy we are shown the necessity
> in transcending our finite particularity and viewing things from
> the standpoint of the Idea. . . . From this standpoint it is

encumbent upon the individual to "forget himself" in the sense
of his finite particularity to become disinterested in his personal
existence and absorbed in the Idea.[13]

It is easy to find examples in the writings of Hegel in
which the German philosopher says that the true "royal
road" to Truth is objectivity. In the preface to the *Phenomenology of Mind*, Hegel wrote:

> Among the many consequences that follow from what has been
> said, it is of importance to emphasize that, that knowledge is only
> real and can only be set forth fully in the form of science, in the
> form of system. . . .[14]

From here it is a short step to saying (and Allison cites
this passage) that "the individual must all the more forget
himself, as in fact the very nature of science implies that he
should." [15] What, we might ask, is so unusual about all
this? Don't we, after all, expect a judge to disqualify himself if the prisoner at the bar is his own son? Of course
we do, and the reason we do is that we expect the judge to
do his best to get the truth. His mind cannot be clouded or
turned from the demands of justice by the fact that the de-
fendant is his own flesh and blood. We demand that he be
objective. The true scientist makes every effort to get just
the facts and only those conclusions that can be based upon
them through valid inferences. We expect him to be objective.
Why shouldn't we expect the same of the theologian?

A philosophy professor I once heard of, who regularly
taught a course in the philosophy of religion, one day told
his students that he was, in fact, the ideal teacher for such
a course. The reason, he said, was that he could be objective about religion since he was not committed to *any* faith.
Well, many students agreed with him in this, but a few felt

that this instead disqualified him. To be objective means to be detached, impartial, uninvolved. It is no wonder that Kierkegaard described the "aesthetic" life in these terms. Those few students argued that this may be the proper attitude for examining competing theories in science, but religion just *is* the demand that we be completely involved. Thus, to be objective about it is to misrepresent the entire enterprise. Kierkegaard would have agreed with them.

Allison sees Kierkegaard's *Postscript* as an elaborate parody of Hegel, especially the *Phenomenology*. If we go no further than the table of contents, this seems to be borne out. Book 1 is entitled "The Objective Problem Concerning the Truth of Christianity"; Book 2 is concerned with "The Subjective Problem. . . ." It looks as if S.K. is setting up a Hegelian dialectic; that is, we have the objective problem and then its opposite, the subjective problem. If the pattern is to be followed, we would expect a reconciling of these opposites in some higher unity.

First, though, a word should be said on the objective side. Can we base our hope for an eternal happiness on objective evidence of the truth of the Christian faith? Kierkegaard was philosopher enough to be convinced that logical proofs for the existence of God—whether those of St. Anselm or St. Thomas or Descartes—just don't work. The nineteenth century also saw many attempts to prove that the Bible was historically, literally true. Today it is popular, in some circles, to stage lectures in which physicists or biologists argue that Christianity is really proved by science. Kierkegaard had very little patience with such arguments.

Anyone who knows even a little about logic should be able to understand his reason for rejecting them. One recent logic text (not quite chosen at random) distinguishes between deductive and inductive arguments in the following manner: "Deductive arguments involve the notion of a logically necessary conclusion; statements about matters of fact are probable rather than necessary, and they are confirmed by evidence based upon experience." [16] For Kierkegaard this meant that historical arguments could, at best, only show Christianity to be *probable,* not necessary. Am I to stake all, make my desperate bid for eternal happiness, launch out into the deep, etc., based on a *probability?* Clearly this will not do at all.

> An hypothesis may become more probable by maintaining itself against objectives for three thousand years, but it does not on that account become an eternal truth, adequately decisive for one's eternal happiness. Has not Mohammedanism persisted for twelve hundred years? The guaranty of eighteen centuries, the circumstance that Christianity has interpenetrated all the relations of life has transformed the world. . . . Eighteen centuries have no greater demonstrative force than a single day, in relation to an eternal truth which is to decide my eternal happiness.[17]

We cannot solve our problem by approaching it objectively, it appears; the "speculative point of view" has turned out to be inappropriate in this case. If we turn from the objective to the subjective, we fare no better. To do this would mean treating the problem within Hegel's dialectic, that is, treating the subjective objectively, or trying to create an existential (subjective) *system.* If this sounds quite mad, maybe it is—and may very well be Kierkegaard's point. This also points to the sense in which Allison considers much of the *Postscript* a joke:

> The real purpose of this jest is not to convince the reader of a philosophical or religious truth, but to prevent him from

theorizing, even in an "existential" sense about Christianity, and
instead to help him to come to grips, in the isolation of his own
subjectivity, with the question of what it means to become a
Christian. Thus, far from being a contribution, good, bad or
indifferent, to a philosophy of existence, the *Postscript* emerges
as Kierkegaard's attempt at a *reductio ad absurdum* of any such
enterprise.[18]

This requires clarification. Return for a moment to the
logic class. Many such classes begin by considering this argument (which may go back as far as Aristotle):

> All men are mortal.
> Socrates is a man.
> Therefore, Socrates is mortal.

We can construct a logical system of thought (and remember
that Hegel called his philosophic system a "Logic") to show
how certain known truths are related. We can construct a
system to show that, if we know that all men are mortal (are
they?—do people really *die*, or just fall asleep, or "pass
away"?) and *if* we know that Socrates is a man (not a demon
or a god, or even a woman), *then* it follows necessarily that
Socrates is mortal. What was meant by the logic text quoted
on p. 105 is that deductive arguments (such as the one we
are discussing here) claim *certainty* for their conclusions in
that *if* the premises are true then the conclusion cannot be
false. This is what a logical system can do, and, as S.K.
often tells us, this is what we have in Hegel's philosophy.
Such systems *are* possible, and, S.K. insists, Hegel deserves
full credit for providing us with an extremely elaborate
example. The only trouble is the system cannot tell us what
we most want to know. Retaining our present example, we, as

existing individuals, most want to know whether or not it's really *true* that all men are mortal, so that one day we, you and I, also must die. But the system cannot tell us. Worse yet (and this can become involved) the system is made up of universal truths, but I am only an individual, a particular existing individual, so that *I* am not in the system at all. This is why all attempts to treat the truth of my subjectivity in an objective manner end in absurdities, in nonsense. And this is the reason for S.K.'s conclusion that "an existential system is impossible." [19]

Earlier it was noted that the *Postscript* looked very much like an example of the Hegelian dialectic, and we can be sure that it was so intended. We have the objective side played against its opposite, the subjective, in part 1. If S.K. were to follow the Hegelian model, we would expect to find the two opposites reconciled in some sort of higher unity. But this is not what we find. Part 2 is a long polemic in favor of increased subjectivity. Once more, as in *Either/Or*, S.K. has replaced the Hegelian "both/and" (the notion that the law of contradiction is annulled) with his own exclusive disjunctive, his *Either/Or*. The existing individual, if he seeks to discover for himself the subjective truth of what it means to become a Christian, cannot accomplish this through an objective system. He does not try to build a system in an objective way, nor can he work out a system in a subjective way. Instead he must seek to *become* a Christian with all of his powers mustered to accomplish the task, and this means abandoning system-building entirely.

WAS THE *POSTSCRIPT* LOGICALLY CONFUSED?

Again and again in part 2 of the *Postscript*, S.K. tells us that the only truth of any real importance or interest to the problem of becoming a Christian is subjective truth. It is this inwardness, this passionate interest in one's relation to God, that counts. It is not the truth of propositions, but subjective truth, that matters. The message is repeated again and again.

This notion of subjective truth has not escaped criticism. Some of the harshest barbs are found in an article by Paul Edwards on "Kierkegaard and the 'Truth' of Christianity." Edwards has three major criticisms. First, in speaking of a new type of "truth" we only create confusion. To illustrate, I offer this paraphrase of Edwards's argument and use his example (with minor adjustments): [20]

Like most men (and unlike Albert Einstein) I usually wear socks on my feet, and wear shoes over the socks. I lean toward browns and blacks, and try to wear brown socks with brown shoes, black with black. Now suppose I were to decide to use the word *socks* to refer to what most other English-speaking people call shoes. I suppose there would be nothing *wrong* with that; one of my teachers used to tell his students to "say what you mean, but be careful." So as long as we explain our singularly peculiar usage, then we're all right, aren't we? Well, yes, but, after all, we already have a perfectly good word for shoes (i.e., *shoes*) and therefore do not need another. Further, this strange usage will cause confusion, as when I say, "Blast it! I goofed and went to the office today wearing my brown socks over my black socks." Edwards's point is that this is also the case with "subjective truth"; we don't need another sense of "truth," and this only produces confusion.

Edwards assumes that there is a standard (accepted, known, etc.) meaning for the English word *truth*. I suspect some philosophers would dispute this, claiming that anyone who has taken a course in epistemology (theory of knowledge) would know that we do *not* have a standard (accepted, known, etc.) meaning for *truth*, perhaps citing as evidence for their claim the fact that if we are asked to define *truth*, we may be unable to do it. But here Edwards can be defended. Suppose little Johnny, third-grade student, is taking a "true-false" test; the test has the sentence "Columbus discovered America in 1492" and a blank beside it that Johnny is to fill with "T" or "F." Does anyone really suppose little Johnny would be sent to the head of the class if he persisted in asking, "Whatever could Teacher mean by that?" Or worse, "Sure, all the books say 1492, but I cling to 1495 with all my passionate, innermost being!" Hardly. Let us admit that Edwards has a case; Kierkegaard *is* sometimes confusing. He may have been the archenemy of Hegel, but he shared some of Hegel's faults.

It will be convenient to move on to Edwards's two other major criticisms. S.K. wants us to believe in this doubly paradoxical Christian faith with all our "interest," i.e., all of our passionate inwardness. Edwards quotes S.K. as saying that "precisely in the interest lies the proof," that is, he interprets Kierkegaard as saying that if we can only make Christianity true *for us*, i.e., subjectively true, we have thereby proved it to be true in the ordinary sense, i.e., objectively true. But S.K.'s point seems to be that the question of *my* immortality is, after all, what must matter to me as an existing individual; why should I be interested in immortality in general? Thus, if we look at the entire passage from which Edwards extracted only a few words, S.K. says:

Systematically immortality cannot be proved at all. The fault

does not lie in the proofs, but in the fact that people will not
understand that viewed systematically the whole question is
nonsense, so that instead of seeking outward proofs, one had
better seek to become a little subjective. Immortality is the most
passionate interest of subjectivity; precisely in the interest lies
the proof.[21]

What is meant here? I suspect S.K. has in that last sentence introduced a different, metaphorical (?) sense of
"proof," but the passage *is* unclear. If Kierkegaard *did*
mean that, somehow, my passionate inwardness proves the
Christian doctrine—proves it to be *true*, in the usual sense—
then Edwards is right in saying, as he does, that "the position just sketched is a glaring and horrendous *non sequitur*." [22]
Certainly the position here attributed to S.K. is a *non
sequitur*, and we must admit that there *are* passages in which
Kierkegaard seems to hold some such position.

Edwards's third major criticism is, in some ways, the
opposite of this. There are some passages in which Kierkegaard praises this passionate inwardness to the point that
he seems to be saying that it doesn't matter what a person
believes, so long as he believes it very earnestly. The case
of the Christian and the pagan (discussed in the previous
chapter) can be understood in this way: it is the pagan, not
the Christian, who "prays in truth." Of this view, Edwards
comments:

> We do not have a view that has any resemblance to theology
> or supernaturalism or to the Christianity that Kierkegaard
> evidently wanted to justify in the first place. What we now have
> is a value judgment—a piece of moral or perhaps psychothera-
> peutic advice—which is consistent with the most thoroughgoing
> atheism. We no longer have the claim that there is a God or that
> any of us will enjoy eternal bliss if we behaved in a certain way.
> Instead we have the claim that if we believed these things or

perhaps, like the idol-worshipers, certain other things in the right frame of mind, we would have achieved the highest kind of existence.[23]

Responding to this criticism requires me to say something that may bother some readers. It was once popular, among certain evangelistic groups, to approach people on the street (or wherever) and ask, "Brother, are you a Christian?" I want to say that, in one sense, that's an odd question. The assumption is that the person questioned will reply with something like "No. I'm a Buddhist." Then the evangelist proceeds to "justify" the Christian faith. Two problems are involved. First, most of us nonmissionaries meet few Buddhists (or few Hindus, Zoroastrians, and only a few more Jews); most of the people we meet are already at least nominally Christian. Second, I am not denying that Christians are to *witness* for the faith; what is denied is that we are called upon to prove it, to "justify" it even if we are able to find someone who will say—straight out—that he is *not* a Christian, in any sense of the term. Edwards makes the mistake of assuming that this was Kierkegaard's aim, i.e., to "justify" or prove Christianity; it wasn't. His quarrel with the likes of Grundtvig and Martensen was not that they had not accepted the Christian faith, so that S.K.'s help was needed to "justify" it for them. On the contrary, they thought Christianity could be justified in terms of Hegel's philosophy; it was Kierkegaard who was convinced that this was a mistake. S.K. did not seek to "justify" Christianity; he sought instead to show what being a Christian involved. He was convinced that many of his countrymen had forgotten, and needed to have the way made clear again.

Finally, having replied in this way to Edwards's second and third objections (both of which involve the false as-

sumption that S.K. meant to *justify* the Christian faith) we
should return to the first objection. We can admit that what
Kierkegaard says about subjective truth is sometimes confusing; it is. But is it *really* so new and strange? Of course
we usually speak of statements as being true. However, we
also talk about a *true* friend, about being *true* to our country, etc. A *true* friend is all that a friend should be. It may
be that what S.K. means by subjective truth is related to
this use. He seems to have felt that it is only through trying
to become a Christian with all our passionate inwardness that
we can become truly human. Emil Brunner freely acknowledges his debt to Kierkegaard when he makes use of this
notion, which he calls "truth as encounter."

> To know him [i.e., God] in trustful obedience is not only to
> *know* the truth, but through God's self-communication to *be* in
> it, in the truth that as love is at the same time fellowship. The
> truth about man is founded in the divine humanity of Christ,
> which we apprehend in faith in Christ, the Word of God. This
> is truth as encounter.[24]

Now we have moved from explicating Kierkegaard's religious thought and discussing the various objections that
have been made against it, and begun to discuss his impact
on contemporary theology. This turns out to be a very large
subject, much too large to be exhaustively treated in the
present volume. But a beginning must be made.

VI. A Maker of the
Modern Theological Mind

THE BELATED BEQUEST

In what sense does Kierkegaard deserve to be called a maker of the modern theological mind? This chapter is written to answer that question. Maybe we should begin by saying that for many years it seemed that his influence would be negligible—or nil. His iconoclasm and prophetic dissent were never warmly received in his own day, and his self-appointed task of Socratic gadfly to his society and its Lutheran Church hardly endeared him to his contemporaries. Although he died in 1855, as late as 1900 S.K. was almost unknown outside Scandinavia. That he made no real impression on the theological deliberations of his century can be seen in the fact that nineteenth-century liberal Protestantism simply ignored him. As a case in point, Adolf Harnack's *Essence of Christianity* (one English translation used the title, *What is Christianity?*), published in 1900, makes

no mention of Kierkegaard's discussion of what it means to
be a Christian.

But his day would come. Events would eventually bring
him a sympathetic audience. "There is a bird called the
stormy-petrel," he wrote in his *Journal* (1843), "and that
is what I am; when in a generation storms begin to gather,
individuals of my type appear." [1] Although the storm was
delayed for more than half a century by optimistic idealism,
its force and fury were present at their worst in the First
World War. (Think of that! Our century is such a century
of crisis that we find it hard to imagine that there had never
before been a global, a *"world"* war! Now we have had two of
them, plus Korea, Vietnam, and a continuing series of Arab-
Israeli conflicts.) Experiences which were unique and solitary in S.K.'s century are now widespread, only too common.
Thus he speaks to our age as he could not speak to his own.
Today his popularity is such that, well, the following com-
ment is typical: "Today, more than a hundred years after
his death, we can say without exaggeration that he is one of
the most important philosophers and theologians—if not the
most important—for our time." [2]

While he might be amused, Kierkegaard would not be particularly surprised by his current popularity, for he was
apparently convinced that some day his message would be
heard. With characteristic insight (and just a bit of conceit)
he predicted that his thought would one day be possessed and
admired by the same sort of people who, during his lifetime,
bore the brunt of his scathing attacks. Three years before his
death he wrote "A Sad Reflection" in his *Journal:*

> In one place in a Psalm it is said of the rich man that he
> heaps up treasures with great toil "and knoweth not who shall
> inherit them." So shall I leave behind me, in an intellectual

sense, a capital by no means insignificant—and, alas, I know also who will be my heir. It is he, that figure so exceedingly distasteful to me, he that till now has inherited all that is best and will continue to do so: The Docent, and the Professor.

Yet this also belongs to my suffering as a necessary part of it—to know this and then go calmly on with my endeavor, which will bring me toil and trouble, and the profit of which, in one sense, the Professor will inherit. "In one sense"—for in another sense I take it with me.

Note. And even if the "Professor" should chance to read this, it will not give him pause, will not cause his conscience to smite him, no, this, too will be made the subject of a lecture.[3]

And so it has happened. The very groups (of both professors and parsons) that S.K. condemned for trying to rationalize the Christian faith have now rationalized his message. This man who said, with such fervor, that what counts in Christianity is definitely not a matter of doctrine, has had his own writings treated as basic doctrinal statements.

But we must not digress from the task of discussing Kierkegaard's influence on contemporary theology.

CONTEMPORARY EXISTENTIAL PHILOSOPHERS

We should not turn from philosophy too quickly, because some of the major theological influence of Kierkegaard came through philosophy.

Let us be specific. The three major existentialist philosophers on the contemporary scene are Jean-Paul Sartre, Karl Jaspers and Martin Heidegger. It is perhaps a measure of Sartre's importance that, in the popular mind, existentialism is an atheistic philosophy. Sartre is, of course, an atheist who, though he learned much about the anguish of human existence from S.K., yet refused to join him in a leap of faith. Sartre's views were discussed earlier in this book.

Returning, then, to Jaspers and Heidegger, it is interesting
to note that both were born Catholics. While they clearly are
not theologians, or even especially known as philosophers
of religion, neither are they atheists. His sometimes mystical
tone notwithstanding, Heidegger is basically a technical
(very!) philosopher of Being and has never claimed to be
a Christian. Somewhat more of a religious theist, Jaspers has
even been called "an extreme liberal Protestant," [4] which may
be appropriate if "extreme" is underlined several times. In
any case, these two inheritors of Kierkegaardian insights have
been somewhat more open and amenable to Christian theology and have been sympathetically received by many Christian thinkers.

A brief word on Jaspers (1883–1969) may be enough for
present purposes. He was deeply influenced by Kant, especially in his understanding of human awareness of the phe-
nomenal world, yet he was unequivocally a Kierkegaardian
in his account of the nature of the existing individual. [5]
Jaspers taught philosophy at the University of Heidelberg
prior to World War II, but he was dismissed from his position by the Nazis. The reason for his dismissal was, inci-
dentally, that he did not, in his published work, support
the orthodox Nazi view of the philosophy of Friedrich
Nietzsche—a philosopher Hitler regarded as the patron saint
of his Third Reich. Jaspers showed that Nietzsche simply
did not fit the role. After the war, Jaspers moved to the University of Basel, where Karl Barth was teaching theology.
It may be worth noting that Barth's later evaluations of the
importance of Kierkegaard for our age are almost identical
to Jaspers's judgments. Both men were ambivalent in their
reactions to Kierkegaard. Though favorable to his call for an
inward search, both reacted against other parts of his thought.
In Jaspers's own words,

I adopted his 'concept' of Existence. But I did not become his disciple. His Christianity left me untouched, and in his negative choices—no marriage, no office, no realization in the world; instead a martyr's existence as essential to Christian truth—I sensed the very opposite of everything I loved and wanted, of everything I was willing or unwilling to do. Both this practical negativism and his "religiousness B" with its view of Christian faith as absurd seemed to me the end of historic Christianity as well as the end of philosophical life. It was the more astonishing, all but inexhaustibly stimulating, what Kierkegaard in his honesty managed to see and to say by the way. Today, I felt, there could be no philosophy without him.[6]

In the end, both Jaspers and Barth were too rationalistic to accept Kierkegaard's paradoxes.

But Barth could not escape Kierkegaard's influence, though he tried often enough. This view requires an explanation: Barth was one of the first major Christian theologians to draw inspiration from the Kierkegaardian literature, and he introduced many later theologians to the work of this disturbing Dane.[7] Indeed, Walter Lowrie—the foremost American translator and expositor of Kierkegaard—reports that it was Barth who first directed his attention to Kierkegaard in the late 1920s.[8]

Barth found in Kierkegaard a perspective very much in tune with modern realities. Against the backdrop of a Europe shattered by World War I, this Swiss minister became convinced of the impotence of the liberal Christianity of his day, publishing a commentary, *The Epistle to the Romans*, which, to say the least, greatly disturbed the naively optimistic theological world of 1918. In tones reminiscent of Kierkegaard's rejection of Hegel's idealism, Barth broke with the dominant German historicism and psychologism of his day, and called for a return to the biblical understanding of God's holiness, man's sin, and salvation through faith.

He cried out as S.K. had done a century earlier, for man to "let God be God!"

Even if Barth had not admitted in the preface of his epoch-making work that he owed much to Kierkegaard, the influence would still be unmistakable. Barth had read Kierkegaard before the war, and both the ideas and the spirit of the *Philosophical Fragments* and the *Concluding Unscientific Postscript* are reflected in Barth's criticism of dull institutionalism, in his rejection of excessive theoretical speculation in theology, and in his pessimistic view of man. Three years later, in 1921, Barth published a revised and expanded edition of his *Romans* which was even more existential in orientation, and in which he explicitly noted the influence of Sören Kierkegaard and of Dostoevsky. The dualism of God/man, the idealistic of grace/judgment, and the preoccupation with paradox, clearly link Barth's understanding of Christian faith to that of his Danish forerunner. For both men, "What is important is not what man thinks about God, but what God thinks about man." [9] The evidence leads some interpreters to conclude that Barth's Christology is found in germ in the *Philosophical Fragments* and in *Training in Christianity*. Thus one affirms, "Barth's conception of Revelation and Christology are both, it seems to me, clearly derived from Kierkegaard." [10] Indeed, one of the most prominent features of Barth's theology—the notion of an endless, yawning qualitative difference between God and man—is a page out of Kierkegaard.

Barth later attempted to move away from S.K.'s shadow and to play down the influence the Dane had exerted on his life and thought. By 1932, the year Barth published the first volume of his *Church Dogmatics*, he had largely moved away from descriptions of the Christian faith in terms of

logical contradiction and paradox, and toward a positive
kerygmatic presentation of a Christocentric theology which
emphasized the essential rationality of faith. Believing as he
did, that Christian theology should be free from entanglement
with philosophy, and being especially concerned to guard
against the anguish and uncertainty of a Kierkegaard, Barth
tried to repudiate his connection with existentialism. In a
more recent series of studies on nineteenth-century thought,
he "neglected" to do an essay on Kierkegaard; late in his
life he tended to explain S.K.'s influence in largely negative
terms. "I consider him to be a teacher," Barth wrote, "into
whose school every theologian must go once. Woe to him
who has missed! So long as he does not remain in it or return
to it." [11] This passage, and the article from which it is quoted,
should be compared with the passage quoted above from
Jaspers's "Epilogue—1955."

THE MARBURG EXPERIENCE

As noted above, much (though not all, as the case of
Barth shows) of Kierkegaard's theological influence came
first through the medium of philosophy. Mention has already
been made of the case of Martin Heidegger (b. 1889), whom
many consider the most important philosopher of the postwar
period. This should be developed further. Since we began
discussing Jaspers by discussing his relationship with Nazi
Germany, we could do the same with Heidegger.

There is a problem, however, because Heidegger's position
with respect to the Hitler government is not clear. It is known
that in the early days of Hitler's rise to power, Heidegger
admired him and his National Socialism; he even joined the
Nazi party. Of course there are some people, notably (and

understandably) Jewish authors, who have not forgotten. One of these is Dagobert Runes, editor of the Philosophical Library. In his *Pictorial History of Philosophy*, Runes devotes *one* page to Heidegger. The page is divided into two parts: on the upper left is a picture of Heidegger, with two paragraphs of text beneath, directly opposite is a slightly larger picture of Hitler with the caption "Adolph Hitler, the spiritual father of a New Europe, according to an enthusiastic Heidegger." Directly beneath the picture of Hitler is a smaller picture, with a caption that describes it exactly: "Hitler's elite guard with flamethrowers driving Jewish women and children out of their ghetto hiding places in Warsaw." [12] The message is only too clear; obviously Heidegger would have approved of having Jews rounded up and killed with flamethrowers! Runes has published another book, a small volume with a large swastika on the cover, made up of Runes's translations of speeches made by Heidegger in praise of the Third Reich, and of clippings from the Nazi press on the same topics. [13]

It must be admitted that some of the things Heidegger said when the National Socialists made him Rector of the University of Freiburg in 1933 make us uncomfortable. But Michael Zimmerman has found another side of the story:

> On the other hand, the following points should be noted. At no time did Heidegger allow racist posters and pamphlets to appear at the university; he personally protected from destruction library books by Jewish authors. . . . He was apparently the only professor not to begin classes with the customary salute to Hitler. . . . His classes were constantly harassed . . . by the Gestapo . . . at a time when such activity was extremely dangerous. Heidegger's lectures on Nietzsche [given from 1935–1943] starkly contradicted the distorted, but official, Nazi interpretation of that thinker. [14]

The matter remains unclear. Heidegger resigned his post as Rector, but why was he permitted to continue lecturing, as Jaspers was not? We cannot be certain. Let us put aside historical matters for the moment.

For Heidegger as for Jaspers, Kierkegaard was a liberating inspiration rather than a master to be slavishly followed. In addition to assimilating the thought of such writers as Augustine, Luther, Pascal, and Nietzsche, we know that he also studied Kierkegaard extensively.[15] At first glance, the claim that S.K. was a formative influence on Heidegger may seem strange and exaggerated. At first on a superficial reading, their works seem to reveal vastly differing personal spirits—the one a lofty, poetic prophet, the other a profound technical intellect, though perhaps we should add that, in recent years, Heidegger has attached much greater importance to poetry. In spite of their different orientations and objectives, the two are in agreement that the starting point of any attempt to understand reality is an honest analysis of the human situation. In fact, Heidegger's most significant contribution to both existential philosophy and theology is that of providing categorical structures concerning human existence which can be used for understanding and clearly stating theological affirmations. Thus, his existential analysis of the human predicament provides contemporary theologians with a means of expressing in a formal manner the religious insights which the Bible expresses in terms of stories and concrete historical events. Specifically, Heidegger's concepts of human existence and man's historicity have been adopted as theological tools by Rudolph Bultmann and Paul Tillich, among others.

Here what may seem to be another digression is in order. Philosophers like to talk about what they call "Camelot experiences." In King Arthur's Camelot, the knights of the Round Table "got it all together," as the young people say. Of course, such things never last, but, for a time, Arthur and such noble knights as Sir Lancelot and Sir Galahad made England teem with peace, virtue, chivalry. Odd as it may seem, philosophers get somewhat dewy-eyed when they speak of prewar Vienna and the famed "Vienna Circle," composed of such philosophers as Rudolf Carnap, Otto Neurath, and Moritz Schlick. American philosophers become emotional when they talk of the "Chicago School of Pragmatists" (John Dewey, Edward Scribner Ames, George Herbert Mead, etc.) assembled at the University of Chicago in the early part of this century. Well, we are not surprised to find that philosophers and theologians alike react enthusiastically to the mention of the University of Marburg and the staff assembled there during the 1920s. At the same time (1927) that he was working on his major work of existential analysis, *Being and Time* (*Sein und Zeit*), Heidegger was teaching on the same faculty at Marburg with Bultmann and Tillich. (Heidegger was at Marburg from 1920–1928, Bultmann from 1922–1928; Tillich was there for only three semesters from 1924–1925.) Thus Heidegger's existential influence has been widely felt in Christian theology and, even when sifted through the systems of technical philosophers, the Kierkegaardian lode has proved to be a rich vein for contemporary theology.

To concentrate on Bultmann for a moment, a major stream of Kierkegaardian philosophy flows to Bultmann through the existential analysis of Martin Heidegger. Because he was basically an "existentialist" before he met Heidegger, Bultmann was glad to find in Heidegger's existential categories a perfect conceptual tool for understanding and expressing the gospel. A number of very good readily available sources amplify this view: One such is John Macquarrie's *An Existentialist Theology: a Comparison of Heidegger and Bultmann*; another is a book in this series, *Makers of the Modern Theological Mind: Rudolf Bultmann*, by Morris Ashcraft.[16] We shall therefore be brief in our discussion, but we can still be clear.

Bultmann used Heidegger's insights for two basically different, but related, reasons. Bultmann was convinced that if God is really to speak to modern man, his voice must be heard through a modern philosophy. If at first blush this sounds quite mad, we are forgetting that the idea is nothing new. To cite only one example, if we turn to the Book of Hebrews, we read of the priests here on earth that "they serve a *copy* and *shadow* of the heavenly sanctuary" (8:5, RSV, emphasis mine). Then when God wanted Moses to prepare the tabernacle, we read that he said, "See that you make everything according to the *pattern* which was shown you" (8:5, RSV, emphasis mine). And at the beginning of chapter 10 we are told, "For since the law has but a *shadow* . . . of the *true form* of these realities" (10:1, RSV, emphasis mine).

What is all this about copies, shadows, patterns, and the "true form of these realities"? Bible scholars have their disputes about who wrote the Letter to the Hebrews, nor are they agreed about who "the Hebrews" were. But the best guess is that the book was written to Jews of the dispersion, and this meant that they were Jews living in a Greek culture. Their thought patterns were Greek, so the writer of this book of the Bible spoke to the readers of his day through the medium of Plato's philosophy. The terms cited above would all be familiar to one schooled in Plato's thought. So just as

this writer spoke to his generation through the medium of
Plato's philosophy, today, Bultmann is convinced, we can
better speak—and convey our theology—through the medium
of Heidegger's philosophy.

The second reason for using Heidegger's philosophy can
be stated much more briefly, though to be convinced of it we
would have to read some of Bultmann's work. And of course
we may not be convinced even then. Let us grant that
Heidegger's analyses provide a convenient modern garb for
expressing theological insights; is this the only reason for
using them? Notice that we might, as I once read somewhere,
use Freudian terminology and thought patterns to explain
Shakespeare. We might do this, even if we think Freud was
completely wrong, had a dirty mind, or various other
objections. But people will understand us if we explain
Shakespeare through Freud because they know the work of
Freud. Is this why Bultmann used Heidegger? No, not
entirely: the point is rather that Bultmann believes Heidegger
is more than convenient. Heidegger's philosophy, Bultmann
is convinced, is essentially correct, and is peculiarly well
suited for the transmission of the Christian message. For him
it became *the* key to an existential interpretation of the Bible
—for demythologizing the message of Christ by stripping
away the outmoded cosmology of angels and demons, and
reading the New Testament proclamation of Christ as the
answer to man's existential search of authentic existence.

Where does Kierkegaard fit into all of this? Here
Macquarrie's book is as specific as we could wish.[17] From
Heidegger, Bultmann takes a description of man as living
in anxiety (*Angst*), aware that he faces the threat of non-
being, i.e., death. And where do we find a full discussion of
this anxiety? Well, another name for anxiety is dread—all

spelled out in S.K.'s book, *The Concept of Dread.* In much the same way, Bultmann read in both S.K. and Heidegger that my freedom is sometimes lost, my existence becomes inauthentic, when I am, so to speak, caught in the crowd, unidentified, just doing what others do.

> They have, so to speak, taken away my being, so that I am no longer myself. Yet when I ask who it is that has thus acquired dominance over me, and makes my decisions for me, it turns out to be no one in particular. It is the neuter 'das Man' in Heidegger's terminology, the German impersonal pronoun denoting an indefinite subject of action. We might translate it into English as "people" or "the public" [the expression used by Kierkegaard for the same phenomenon]. . . .[18]

We could give other examples, but Macquarrie and Ashcraft have already done this, and done it well. The only point to be emphasized here is that we can trace the categories used to express Bultmann's theology back to the philosophy of Heidegger, and often we can trace these categories back to Kierkegaard.

Another major source of Bultmann's readily acknowledged debt to S.K. is his early identification with the dialectical theology of Barth, Brunner and Gogarten in rejecting the nineteenth-century liberalism which as students they had all inherited and accepted. Bultmann's view of the great gap separating God and man, his conception of revelation as personal encounter, his understanding of faith not as proof but as risk, his view of man as a "chooser"—all of these emphases reveal his debt to Kierkegaard. Overshadowing these affinities, however, is a seemingly irreconcilable difference in perspective. Although he was outspoken in his dissent and often unorthodox in his life, still S.K. was basically a conservative gadfly. Taking his stand against the "enlight-

ened" reason of his age, he sought to recover what he thought
was the simple but demanding faith of the New Testament—
a New Testament which, especially in his later years, he
unquestioningly assumed to be literally true, and which he
interpreted ascetically.

Bultmann, on the other hand, had studied with such
biblical scholars as Gunkel, Julicher, and Weiss; and while
he became convinced of the inadequacy of much of liberalism, he was fully committed to an ongoing critical study of
the New Testament. Indeed, Bultmann pioneered in the
"form" critical study of the New Testament—a radical
criticism which in his hands often led to conclusions skeptical
of the historical reliability of much New Testament testimony
about Jesus of Nazareth. Bultmann's thought is therefore
obviously not a carbon copy of S.K.'s. As one looks at the
great gulf which separates the two, one may wonder what
brings these two together in an existential understanding of
the gospel. The answer emphasizes a significant point in their
relationship. They were both struggling with the same crucial
question—"How is faith related to historically uncertain
facts?" [19]

For both men the question arose in response to the general
cultural and intellectual climate in which they lived, a
climate that pitted science and reason against traditional
Christianity. The revolution in Western man's thinking which
accompanied the Enlightenment encouraged the increasing
application of historical-critical methods to the Bible.
Kierkegaard observed the "attacks" of biblical criticism and
the "defense" of orthodoxy with impatient disdain; in his
eyes *both* sides were missing the points. Thus he could ask:

Can one learn anything from history about Christ? No. Why

not? Because one can "know" nothing at all about "Christ";
He is the paradox. . . . About him nothing can be known, he
can only be believed.[20]

Consequently, when nearly a century later Bultmann
found himself struggling with the same issue, he discovered
that a Kierkegaardian understanding of faith actually freed
him to do his critical work without the fear of endangering
theology—for the gospel was to be understood in existential
rather than historical categories. Bultmann is most fully a
Kierkegaardian in his rejection of historical categories. "It
is only when there is no objective guarantee," he argues,
"that faith acquires meaning and strength, for only then is
it authentic decision." [21]

Finally, Bultmann's Christian ethic owes a great deal to
Kierkegaard. His ethic has been described as an ethic of
"radical obedience" wherein one listens for and responds to
the Word of God speaking through the situation in which he
exists. In this basic posture, and in many of the details of
his position, his debts to S.K. are, once more, very evident.
Kierkegaard's *Works of Love* shines through Bultmann's
understanding of love, and his view of obedience is clearly
related to S.K.'s *Fear and Trembling*.[22] Following Kierkegaard's dictum that "an existential system is impossible" and
his interpretation of the great commandment "Love thy
neighbor as thyself," Bultmann develops an existential ethic
(not a system!) whose only content is to act in love. In
Bultmann's words,

> The demand of the moral good is not made evident to me in
> a system, or an ideal, but confronts me concretely in my meeting
> with the neighbor. Who is my neighbor? And what must I do
> for him? This I must perceive for myself at any given time,
> and it is in love that I am able to do so.[23]

PAUL TILLICH AND OTHERS

With Paul Tillich, the Kierkegaardian revolution has come full circle. With Tillich, religious existentialism has taken its largest step away from a perspective characterized —at least by its detractors—as subjective irrationalism, and toward a reasoned systematic conceptualization of the Christ in faith. The protests of S.K.'s *Postscript* notwithstanding, Tillich has shown that an existential thinker *can* have a system. He even goes so far as to claim that metaphysics (or 'ontology', as he and Heidegger prefer to call it in order to avoid the unfortunate connotation of 'metaphysics' as dealing with transempirical realities) is a proper and a necessary task for theology. Tillich, however, is certainly not a pure-blooded German idealist. In his view, the genetic defect inherent in that tradition has come to him healed by the correctives of Schelling, Kierkegaard, Marx, and Nietzsche. As a young theology student, unhappy with what he took to be the hollowness of Ritschlian liberalism, yet unwilling to retreat into an uncritical conservatism, Tillich was "extremely happy" when he encountered Kierkegaard:

> I recall with pride how as students of theology at Halle we came into contact with Kierkegaard's thought through translations made by an isolated individual in Württemberg. In the years 1905–1907 we were grasped by Kierkegaard. It was a great experience.[24]

It was the "confirmation of intense piety" which went to the depths of human existence "and the philosophical greatness which he had received from Hegel" [25] (!?) that made S.K. so important for the young Tillich. Even so, the full impact of S.K.'s existentialism would not be felt by

Tillich until some twenty years later. According to Tillich himself this first encounter with Kierkegaard made little impact, "for the spirit of the nineteenth century still prevailed, and we hoped that the great synthesis between Christianity and humanism could be achieved with the tools of German classical philosophy." [26]

Intellectually, it was World War I (in which Tillich served four years as a chaplain) which finally brought the nineteenth century to a close. In the wake of that disaster a growing number of European thinkers—especially in Germany—were beginning to think that Kierkegaard's seemingly wild and irrational assertions just might turn out to be true. Because of his earlier encounters with the works of Kierkegaard and Nietzsche, Tillich was well prepared for the philosophic shift which was to come during his three semesters of teaching at Marburg. While there, Tillich turned more and more to the existential posture which was being rediscovered in his Kierkegaardian revival:

> In Marburg, in 1925, I began work on my *Systematic Theology*
> . . . at the same time that Heidegger was in Marburg as professor
> of philosophy, influencing some of the best students, existentialism
> in its twentieth century form crossed my path. It took years
> before I became fully aware of the impact of this encounter on
> my own thinking. I resisted, I tried to learn, I accepted the new
> way of thinking more than the answers it gave.[27]

The question could be raised as to whether S.K. or Heidegger had the greater impact on Tillich, but to do so would be to miss the point. Tillich found the existential perspective which had been worked out by S.K. and further developed by Heidegger to be most helpful in coming to grips with the meaning of human life. S.K. and Heidegger had woven a tapestry which portrays man living in estrangement in anxious finitude, guilt and despair, suffering from the Sickness unto Death. And the existential analysis of man's predicament which is so central to Tillich's thought is cut from the same cloth. The Tillichian emphasis on man as finite freedom, and the resulting importance of individual decision, is also closely akin to the thought of these men. Even the description of faith as "ultimate concern," certainly one of the key insights in Tillich's system, is intimately related to Kierkegaard's emphasis on the nature of religious knowledge, wherein one is "grasped by the ultimate." Thus Tillich describes the object of religion (and theology) with explicit reference to Kierkegaard, as "the object of total surrender demanding also the surrender of our subjectivity while we look at it. It is a matter of infinite passion and interest (Kierkegaard), making us its object whenever we try to make it our object." [28]

As the religious tone of this quote begins to reveal, not all of the Kierkegaardian influence on Tillich came through Heidegger. As with Bultmann, other aspects of Kierkegaardian influence came through Tillich's early identification with the "dialectical" theology pioneered by Barth. In the early twenties (1923–24), Tillich entered into an extended discussion with Barth and Gogarten in which he (Tillich) took his stand with Barth, Kierkegaard, Pascal, Luther, and others, "against every 'immediate, unparadoxical relation to the Unconditioned' which turns the unapproachable divine Majesty into a finite idol." [29]

Indeed, several thoroughly Barthian (and Kierkegaardian) emphases which were never repudiated appear in Tillich's early writings. Among these are his description of the gulf which separates man and God, the absolute need for divine revelation, and the inevitability of paradox when using human language to express divine revelation.

This double lineage to Kierkegaard through Heidegger's philosophy on the one hand and through dialectical theology on the other points to an insight which was implied in Bultmann's theology but which is explicit and conscious in Tillich's system. Tillich's "method of correlation" is based on his belief that philosophy asks the questions about existence which theology must answer. The most searching questions of our day are those posed by the framework of existential analysis, but the answers come from biblical religion. To give only one example, the problem of man's estrangement is answered by the power of the New Being in Christ. Always the questions without the answers are incomplete, and often the answers without the questions are meaningless. Man's existential questions and the gospel's answers must be correlated, and this is what Tillich tried to do in all his works, but especially in his three-volume *Systematic Theology*.

This is not the place for a full treatment of the theology of Paul Tillich, and none is attempted here. We have been able to show that he was influenced by Kierkegaard. Along the way we also discussed Kierkegaard's influence on Jaspers and Heidegger, and Barth and Bultmann. Surely this is more than we need to show that S.K. deserves a high ranking among the "Makers of the Modern Theological Mind."

The problem is knowing when to stop. In chapter 3 mention was made of Martin Buber's discussion of the "teleological suspension of the ethical." Much more could be said about Kierkegaard's influence on Buber, and through him, on Jewish thought in general.[30] We could, at the other end of the spectrum, discuss the influence of Kierkegaard on Roman Catholic thought as reflected in the work of Gabriel Marcel.[31] It would be very interesting to trace the often-acknowledged impact of Kierkegaard on the writings

of another Protestant theologian, Emil Brunner; we can find
many references to Kierkegaard in Brunner's works on ethics
and on the place of revelation in Christian theology.[32]
Finally, we could enlarge on the fact that Reinhold Niebuhr
began to wrestle with problems of theological anthropology
—which problems developed into his work on the *Nature
and Destiny of Man*—at the very time he discovered
Kierkegaard.[33]

"Finally," we said, but this is final only because we make
it so. And we must make it so, because the truth that begins
to emerge is that modern theology just wouldn't be what it
is today had there been no Kierkegaard. His influence was
so immense and so far-reaching that a thorough treatment of
it would involve nothing less than a thorough, and detailed,
examination of virtually all aspects of modern theology—
and *that*, surely, is beyond the scope of the present volume.

Conclusion

A writer should try to be clear throughout his work. If he is, there is really no need to pause near the end for a final summary, or a final evaluation. But sometimes it is difficult to keep an entire book in mind, and view it all at once. This book is not as long as some, but perhaps it is long enough to justify a final summary and an evaluation of its subject.

Most of Kierkegaard's principal philosophical and theological insights are found in his discussions of the three spheres of existence. The aesthetic sphere is his parody of the Hegelian philosophers. The major point is that this philosopher is a mere spectator of life, not a participant. He spins theories but does not see that a choice is demanded.

There is really very little that is new in Kierkegaard's discussion of ethical theory.[1] Kierkegaard makes only minor changes in the theory of Immanuel Kant; the changes are intended to emphasize the fact that our duties are often derived from the roles we play in society. Essentially, Kierkegaard was concerned to show that the ethical man can always defend himself rationally. By contrast, the religious man *cannot* defend himself rationally. Perhaps the most interesting part of Kierkegaard's philosophy, for many people, is his claim that there is a "teleological suspension of the ethical," a higher call in relation to which the moral law has to be, as it were, suspended. But though the religious man acknowledges that he hears the call of God, he can never prove to others that his obedience is fully rational. The case of the Christian is particularly perilous, since his religious beliefs often seem contradictory and absurd. Much of Kierkegaard's work is devoted to describing the agony, the anguish, the "fear and trembling" involved in the "leap of faith" with which a man accepts the call and chooses to lead the Christian life, seemingly against all reason.

Kierkegaard has often been charged with irrationalism. It is claimed that he intended that we should literally *believe* something that we also knew to be self-contradictory. But can we even make sense of the notion of believing a contradiction? I once thought it possible to show this charge to be false; I still think that a close examination of the subject and the relevant texts deserves a verdict of "not proved."

As has been stated often in the preceding chapters, we must keep in mind (and this is more true of Kierkegaard than any writer I know) the author's intended audience. Kierkegaard wrote about what it means to become a Christian. He lived in a country in which people became Christians just by being born; this was a country with a state church. Thus there was nothing difficult about becoming a Christian, certainly, and nothing very tough about living as one. The clergy, especially, did very well (they wore fine clothes, lived in large houses, had large salaries). Further, while Christianity seemed so paradoxical to him, to them it was all clear, easily worked out with a little help from the Hegelian philosophy. It is the main contention of the present book that S.K.'s work can best be understood as a sustained polemic against the easy, "rational" religion that he saw— or *thought* he saw; I do not mean to imply that he was correct —in the Danish Lutheran Church of his day. He wrote *against* this church, as he saw it, and he may have overstated his case. The point is he should not be criticized for failing to do what in fact he had no intention of doing.

Suppose, however, someone were to ask: "But why should I read Kierkegaard today? I'm not a nineteenth-century Danish Lutheran and, besides, I don't like writers who are so *negative* about everything." A good evaluation of Kierkegaard should try to answer such questions. We could begin by asking, as I did earlier, are our churches today so very different? Don't we still have many of the same problems? Don't we still, very often, take our faith too lightly? Further, as amply demonstrated in chapter 6, it is difficult to see how we could understand contemporary theology without reading Kierkegaard, since so much of our current religious thought (and of course, much of our current philosophy) is based on his writings.

As to the charge that S.K. was overly negative, there are two sides to that coin. On the one side, is it always bad to be negative? Sometimes we want so very much to get along with people that we get the idea that we should never disagree with anyone. Sometimes we like to emphasize the fact that, as the prefix *pro* would suggest, the "protestant" is really *for* certain things. That's true enough, but when Luther put those theses on the church door and said, "Here I stand; I cannot do otherwise," he was being negative. He was *against* certain things, and thought he had a right, and even a duty, to be against them. Sometimes we have to say "No!" and say it emphatically. Christians over the centuries have given their lives for their faiths, frequently as a penalty for saying "No." Kierkegaard's "no" may also have cost him his life. Whether or not he was right the reader must decide, but what he did was in the best Protestant tradition.

The other side of the coin is that, while we must sometimes be negative, we should not stop there. Suppose we do, finally, not only fight the system and the "establishment," but fight them and *win*? "Come the revolution, we'll throw the rascals out and take over. . . . Then what?" As noted in chapter 6, more than one contemporary theologian (and more than one philosopher) read Kierkegaard, profited from the experience, and then moved on. For all of his greatness, Kierkegaard's work *was* primarily negative. Kant said that the Scottish philosopher David Hume woke him from his dogmatic slumbers; this is a much-needed service that Kierkegaard has provided for many readers. But we should not try to be his disciples, or accept his views as our own, without critical examination. He certainly said often enough that he never wanted anyone to do that. Put very simply, he wanted us to think for ourselves and make our own decisions. He wanted no disciples. In the end, the desire of his heart was that we should become Christians, not Kierkegaardians.

Bibliographical Essay

Lists of the published works of Sören Kierkegaard are readily available, and most of the major works have been cited or discussed in the preceding chapters, so the reader could easily prepare his own list. Since the story of how Kierkegaard became known to English-speaking readers is almost as interesting as his life story, the major concern of this essay will be with secondary sources.

If only Kierkegaard had written in English, or German, or even French, there is little doubt that he would have been world-famous fifty years earlier. But he wrote Danish, and the miracle is that he became known at all. Danish is simply not spoken by that many people.

Remember that Kierkegaard died in 1855. I have already mentioned (in chapter 2) the name of Harald Höffding, a Danish scholar who should be recognized by many philosophy majors because of his *History of Modern Philosophy* and his

Philosophy of Religion. He also wrote a book on Kierkegaard
in 1892 which was translated into German as *Sören Kierkegaard als Philosoph (S.K. as Philosopher)* in 1896 (Fr.
Frommans Verlag, Stuttgart). This book did much to make
Kierkegaard known on the continent. The earliest reference
to S.K. that I have found in English is a review of Höffding's
book in *The Monist* in that same year of 1896. Thomas J.
McCormack, the translator of Ernest Mach's scientific works
and assistant editor of *The Monist* (Paul Carus was the editor) wrote the review. He seems to have understood Kierkegaard as he wrote of him:

> . . . a commanding figure in Danish life and thought, little known
> outside the boundaries of his native country. . . . His works are
> numerous and bear mainly upon the burning ethical problems of
> existence. They have all an intensely practical bearing, and, in
> style, the incisive forcefulness which comes from straightforward
> and honest effort. His prose, direct, homely, and vivid, joined to
> great persuasive power, wealth of metaphor, satire, and invective,
> stands unrivalled in Danish literature. . . . His interests were
> never purely theoretical or scientific, but ethical, educational, and
> salvational. . . . Some of his work has been translated into Ger-
> man.[1]

Again, *none* of his work, so far as I can discover, was
available in English, and this 1896 reference is the earliest I
have found. Apparently this early reference attracted no attention.

Two years later, in 1898, a young assistant at the University of Minnesota browsing through a local library was attracted to an unusual volume. The book was in Danish. It
happened that the young man, a Swede, could read Danish,
and he found that he was unable to put the book down. He
was so intrigued that he read all night that night and finished

the book within twenty-four hours. The book was Kierkegaard's *Concluding Unscientific Postscript;* the young man was David F. Swenson. Convinced, apparently at once, of the genius of Kierkegaard, he began to read S.K.'s other works, everything by him that he could put his hands on. It is reported that

in 1914, in a course sponsored by the University of Minnesota on "Great Thinkers of the Nineteenth Century" he gave his first public address on Kierkegaard. This was, I believe, the first public address on Kierkegaard ever delivered in this country.[2]

In July 1916, Swenson published an article in the *Philosophical Review* introducing Kierkegaard to the American reader. Entitled "The Anti-intellectualism of Kierkegaard," [3] it remains one of the best general works on Kierkegaard, truly a pioneering effort. Swenson also wrote an excellent book on Kierkegaard, with the modest title *Something About Kierkegaard.*[4]

It is probable that the first English translation of selections from Kierkegaard's work was by Professor Lee M. Hollander of the University of Texas, published by the University of Texas in 1923 as Bulletin No. 1226, Comparative Literature Series, No. 3. Since this fact is so little known, Professor David L. Miller, also of the University of Texas, Austin, asked that Professor Hollander relate the details. Professor Miller has graciously given his permission to publish Hollander's description of how he came to publish the first translations of Kierkegaard in English:

To the best of my recollection I first became acquainted with the writings of Kierkegaard when I was studying at the University of Oslo, directly after Norway and Sweden amicably agreed to separate (1905). Though primarily interested in the study of Old Norse and attending lectures at the University I began to read Scandinavian literature extensively. One day I strolled over into the east side of that fascinating city, which had just changed its name from Christiana to Oslo, and came to the so-called Deichmannske Bibliotech. This is a private collection, open to everybody, where one is allowed to browse along open stacks, and charge out books and Journals. In doing so I came across volumes of Kierkegaard's writings, and quickly became fascinated by the man's unusual style in expressing original ideas. Subsequently, after accepting an instructorship at the University of Michigan, I found the leisure to translate some of his writings. . . . These I offered to a number of publishers, without success, of course, for S.K. was at that time unknown in English-speaking countries, though some of his works had been translated into German. So the Ms. reposed in my desk. In 1911 I transferred to the University of Texas. One hot afternoon, I was swimming with my friend Howard M. Jones of the Department of English (later, Professor of English and Comparative Literature at Harvard), and when resting he asked me if I had anything which he could publish in the Bulletins of which he was editor. After reading what I called "Selections from the Writings of S.K." he enthusiastically gave it to the imprimatur. Coming out unbound it received no review whatever, and being sent to all newspaper editors of the state, promptly went into their wastepaper baskets, I am sure. But a few years ago my friend, Professor David Miller, of the Department of Philosophy, on a walk asked me whether I had any spare copies of the book, and as I had not, suggested that I republish it as a paperback. The first publisher I sent it to, Doubleday & Co., promptly accepted it—S.K., by that time, owing to Sartre, had become well known. *Habent sua fata libelli.*

Professor Hollander's *Selections* are now available as a convenient paperback, published by Doubleday Anchor Books (Garden City, N.Y.).

Kierkegaard's influence spread slowly. In 1929, Professor William K. Stewart of Dartmouth wrote an article on the place of paradoxes in religious thought, in which he said of S.K.:

Kierkegaard, with his inexorable alternative "Either/Or," has been oftenest remembered as the prototype of Ibsen's *Brand*, but it would seem that his real intellectual influence has only just begun. In some strange fashion he has penetrated into Spain and has found an enthusiastic admirer in Unamuno. Also the most striking figures in recent German theological thought, Rudolf Otto and Karl Barth, bear unmistakably his impress. He is the relentless foe of ease in Zion, of lukewarmness and mere institutionalism and, above all, of that pseudo-religion which consists in making the best of both worlds. Surely no religious leader in modern times has essayed so vehemently to live and think by paradox alone.[5]

We can see from what Professor Stewart wrote above (concerning Barth, Otto and Unamuno) that Kierkegaard's influence was increasing on the continent. This is confirmed by other sources. In 1931, Arthur Liebert reported on "Contemporary European Philosophy" to his American readers:

But the man who has been especially influential in restoring the eros for religion to life among us is the great Dane Sören Kierkegaard. In the present trend towards religious revival, it is natural and right that this profound and passionately upright fighter should be on thousands of lips, and that his writings should obtain a great following.[6]

We should also mention the useful introduction to S.K. which Edward Geismar wrote in 1929—a fine, basic early introduction in an article for the *American-Scandinavian Review*.[7] Geismar is also responsible for two of the better early books, *Sören Kierkegaard* (1937), and *Lectures on the Religious Thought of Sören Kierkegaard* (1938) both published by the Augsburg Publishing House, Minneapolis.

But Kierkegaard was still largely unknown in this country when Dr. Walter Lowrie wrote his monumental *Kierkegaard* in 1938 (Oxford University Press, London).[8] The great value of this work was its thoroughness. It is primarily biographical, with illustrations, and it interpreted S.K.'s thought in an

extremely competent fashion. Since not very much of Kierkegaard's work was readily available in English, Lowrie translated lengthy passages, thus singlehandedly making S.K.
available to the English reader as he had not been before.

Swenson and Lowrie are actually both better known as
translators. Swenson began the work of translating Kierkegaard, completing the translation of the *Philosophical
Fragments* but leaving unfinished his translation of *Concluding Unscientific Postscript*, when he died in 1940. Lowrie
completed that task and also translated most of Kierkegaard's
other works, an incredibly long list altogether. It is not item-
ized here because Lowrie has discussed his work himself in
two separate papers: "How Kierkegaard got into English,"
appended to his translation of Kierkegaard's *Repetition*
(Princeton University Press, 1946) and "Translators and Interpreters of S.K." in the October 1955 issue of *Theology
Today*. That entire issue of *Theology Today* will interest the
reader, since it was a centenary number devoted to articles on
Kierkegaard and includes such papers as "Grundtvig and
Kierkegaard: Their Views of the Church" by Henning Hoirup
and "Theological and Philosophical Kierkegaardian Studies
in Scandinavia, 1945–1953" by Niels Thalstrup. By 1942
enough of S.K.'s work had been translated that Lowrie could
publish his *Short Life of Kierkegaard* (Princeton University
Press), excluding many of the long quotes from S.K. which
he had had to include in the longer *Kierkegaard.*

From the forties up to the present day, Kierkegaard has
become increasingly popular, so we must be more selective
in listing sources. Of the several anthologies available now,
none is better than *A Kierkegaard Anthology* by Robert Bretall. This anthology has liberal selections from all major
works of S.K., and an excellent bibliography. It was first

published by the Princeton University Press in 1946, and is now available in a Modern Library edition.

Turning again to periodicals, I shall limit myself to one author only in philosophy and one theological writer. On the philosophy side, Louis Mackey has a distinguished series of papers, four of which appeared in the *Review of Metaphysics:* "Kierkegaard and the Problem of Existential Philosophy," part 1 in March 1956, part 2 in June 1956; "The Loss of the World in Kierkegaard's Ethics" in June 1962; and "Philosophy and Poetry in Kierkegaard" in December 1969. A fifth, "Some Versions of the Aesthetic: Kierkegaard's *Either/Or*," appeared in the Winter 1964 issue of *Rice University Studies.* This series of papers has resulted in Professor Mackey's recent book, *Kierkegaard: A Kind of Poet* (University of Pennsylvania Press, Philadelphia, 1971). On the religious side, the best author may be Paul L. Holmer. Again, we can cite five papers: "Kierkegaard, a Religious Author" in the *American-Scandinavian Review* for June 1945; "Kierkegaard and Ethical Theory" in *Ethics* for April 1953; "Kierkegaard and Religious Propositions" in the *Journal of Religion* for July 1955, "Kierkegaard and the Sermon" in the *Journal of Religion* for January 1957; and "Kierkegaard and Theology" in the *Union Theological Seminary Quarterly Review* for March 1957. Jerry H. Gill has recently published a very good, well-rounded collection of papers on S.K., mostly from periodicals, under the title *Essays on Kierkegaard* (Burgess Publishing Company, Minneapolis, 1969). Even more recently, Josiah Thompson has edited his *Kierkegaard: A Collection of Critical Essays* (Doubleday Anchor Books, 1972), which features a very useful bibliography of books and articles on S.K. in English from 1956–70. If I were teaching a course on S.K. and could use only a limited number of books, I would

use the Bretall anthology for S.K.'s own works, and the
Thompson volume for secondary sources—and, needless to
say, I'd insist the students buy my book.

A final word about books. I don't think that the early
works of Swenson, Lowrie, and Geismar have been surpassed.
They're still good. As I indicated in the text above (chapter
3), I consider the best general work on Kierkegaard to be *The
Mind of Kierkegaard* by James Collins (Henry Regnery Co.,
Chicago, 1953). Mention should also be made of a book
somewhat similar to the present volume, *The Promise of
Kierkegaard* by William Hamilton (J. B. Lippincott Co.,
Philadelphia, 1969). Again, many other books could be
listed, but none better than these.

General introductions to existentialism usually contain a
chapter on Kierkegaard. There are literally dozens of these,
but five such volumes deserve specific mention: *Irrational
Man: A Study in Existential Philosophy* by Willam Barrett
(Doubleday Anchor Books, 1958); *The Challenge of Existentialism* by John Wild (Indiana University Press, Blooming-
ton, 1955); *Existentialism and the Modern Predicament* by
F. H. Heinemann (Harper & Row, New York, 1958); *Existentialism and Religious Belief* by David E. Roberts (Oxford
University Press, New York, 1959) which has two chapters
on S.K.; and *Christianity and the Existentialists*, edited by
Carl Michalson (Charles Scribner's Sons, New York, 1956),
in which an item of special interest is the paper on S.K. by H.
Richard Niebuhr.

We should close with the usual "legal disclaimer" that, of
course, secondary sources are no substitute for originals.
Certainly we should read Kierkegaard's own words first, in
the original Danish, if possible. But few Americans speak
Danish, and sometimes making sense of Kierkegaard in En-

glish is difficult enough. In this case, the reader is surely justified in using secondary sources; I only hope that I have
pointed the way to some of the better ones. My ultimate hope
is that I can help the reader enjoy his study of Kierkegaard.
It is an ancient adage (from Horace, I believe) that we should
seek to mingle profit with delight. Perhaps I shall fail in
making a study of Kierkegaard *delightful*—though his wit
will help me in this—but I am confident that anyone will
profit from reading his work. Perhaps that is enough, for I
am also convinced that reading him will be more than simply
intellectually profitable; he can point the way to make us
better men. Remember that his aim was to help us to become
Christians.

Another "Concluding Unscientific Postscript"

Writing a book on Kierkegaard is frustrating because the feeling—mentioned above—persists that Kierkegaard said it better. The authors therefore wish to "conclude" this book with one more quotation from Kierkegaard, a prayer this time, which sums up his work and thought as well as any passage we know:

> God in heaven, I thank Thee that Thou hast not required it of man that he should comprehend Christianity; for if that were required, I should be of all men the most miserable. The more I seek to comprehend it, the more incomprehensible it appears to me, and the more I discover merely the possibility of offense. Therefore, I thank Thee that Thou dost only require faith, and I pray Thee to increase it more and more.[1]

Amen.

Notes

CHAPTER I

1. Sören Kierkegaard, *Philosophical Fragments* (New York: Princeton University Press, 1958), p. 3.
2. Ronald Grimsley, *Kierkegaard: A Biographical Introduction* (New York: Charles Scribner's Sons, 1973), p. 55.
3. Alexander Dru, ed., *The Journals of Kierkegaard* (New York: Harper Torchbooks, 1959), p. 169.
4. Ibid., p. 252.
5. Ibid., p. 253.
6. Sören Kierkegaard, *Attack Upon Christendom* (Boston: Beacon Press, 1957), p. 60.
7. Rolf Hochhuth, *The Deputy* (New York: Grove Press, 1964), p. 219.
8. Walter Kaufmann, *Religion From Tolstoy to Camus* (New York: Harper Torchbooks, 1964), p. 34.
9. Ibid.
10. Kierkegaard, *Attack Upon Christendom*, p. 164.
11. Ronald Gregor Smith, "Kierkegaard's Library," *The Hibbert Journal* 50, no. 196 (October 1951): 18–21.

CHAPTER II

1. Sören Kierkegaard, *Either/Or*, 2 vols. (Garden City, N.Y.: Doubleday, Anchor Books, 1959), 1:301.
2. Ibid., p. 25.
3. Ibid., p. 35.
4. Ibid., p. 28.
5. Ibid., p. 24.
6. Ibid., p. 27.
7. Ibid.. p. 36.
8. Ibid., p. 280.
9. Ibid., p. 281.
10. Ibid., p. 293.
11. Ibid., p. 98.
12. Ibid., pp. 303–4.
13. Robert Bretall, ed., *A Kierkegaard Anthology* (New York: Modern Library, 1959), p. 20.
14. Kierkegaard, *Either/Or*, 1:9.
15. Ibid., p. 447.
16. Ibid.
17. Ibid.
18. Ibid., p. 328.
19. Ibid., p. 332.
20. Ibid., p. 338.
21. Ibid., p. 341.
22. Ibid., p. 368.
23. Ibid., p. 430.
24. Ibid., p. 304.
25. Kierkegaard, *Either/Or*, 2:7.
26. Ibid., p. 163.
27. Ibid., p. 173. See also pp. 170, 172.
28. Ibid., p. 171.
29. Ibid., pp. 169–70.
30. Ibid., p. 174.
31. A good book to read in this connection is W. T. Stace's *The Philosophy of Hegel* (New York: Dover, 1955). Stace's interpretation of Hegel's philosophy may be and has been questioned. But the book is helpful because Stace interprets Hegel exactly as Kierkegaard interpreted him, so he can illuminate S.K.'s criticisms.
32. Immanuel Kant, *Critique of Pure Reason*, trans. Norman Kemp Smith, abr. ed. (London: Macmillan, 1952), p. 61.
33. Kierkegaard, *Either/Or*, 2:175–76.
34. William Barrett, *Irrational Man: A Study in Existential Philosophy* (Garden City, N.Y.: Doubleday, 1958), p. 146.
35. Kierkegaard, *Either/Or*, 2:175.

36. Harald Höffding, *A History of Modern Philosophy*, 2 vols. (New York: Dover, 1955), 2:178.

37. Dru, *The Journals of Kierkegaard*, p. 98.

38. Most of the material in the next few pages is from my paper, "Something about Sartre," *The University of Houston Forum* 6, no. 1 (Fall–Winter 1968) : 22–24.

39. Jean-Paul Sartre, *Being and Nothingness* (New York: Philosophical Library, 1956), p. lxvi.

40. Jean-Paul Sartre, *Nausea* (Norfolk, Conn.: New Directions, 1959), p. 37.

41. Ibid., p. 131.

42. Ibid., p. 176.

43. Joseph-Emile Muller, *Modern Painting from Monet to Mondrian* (New York: Castle Books, 1960), p. 21.

44. Sartre, *Being and Nothingness*, p. 79.

45. The short story is reproduced in Walter Kaufmann's anthology, *Existentialism from Dostoevsky to Sartre* (New York: Meridian Books, 1957), pp. 223–40.

46. Sartre, *Being and Nothingness*, p. 33.

47. Iris Murdoch, *Sartre: Romantic Rationalist* (New Haven: Yale University Press, 1959), p. 10.

48. Jean-Paul Sartre, *No Exit and Three Other Plays* (New York: Vintage Books, 1959), p. 47.

49. Sartre, *Being and Nothingness*, p. 90.

50. See Sartre's "Existentialism is a Humanism" in the Kaufmann volume, especially pages 289–92.

CHAPTER III

1. Kierkegaard, *Either/Or*, 2:161.

2. Ibid., p. 217.

3. Paul L. Holmer, "Kierkegaard and Ethical Theory," *Ethics* 63, no. 3, part 1 (April 1953) : 165.

4. Kierkegaard, *Either/Or*, 2:223.

5. Ibid., p. 258.

6. Ibid., p. 147.

7. Ibid., p. 59.

8. For a more detailed treatment of such examples see Miodrag S. Lukich and Elmer H. Duncan, "Kant's Rigorism: A Problem and a Solution," *The Southern Journal of Philosophy* 3, no. 4 (Winter 1965) : 188–91.

9. Kierkegaard, *Either/Or*, 2:328–29.

10. See F. H. Bradley, *Ethical Studies*, 2nd ed. (London: Oxford University Press, 1927).

11. Sören Kierkegaard, *Fear and Trembling* (Garden City, N.Y.: Doubleday, 1954), p. 67.

12. Jean Wahl, *Études Kierkegaardiennes*, 2nd ed. (Paris: J. Vrin, Libraire Philosophique, 1949), p. 190 [my translation].

13. This interpretation of Kant is not standard. The article I co-authored with Lukich is in defense of it. See note 8.

14. Immanuel Kant, *Religion Within the Limits of Reason Alone* (New York: Harper and Brothers, 1960), p. 175.

15. Geoffrey Clive, *The Romantic Enlightenment* (New York: Meridian Books, 1960), p. 152.

16. See my article "Kierkegaard's Teleological Suspension of the Ethical: A Study of Exception Cases," in *The Southern Journal of Philosophy* 1, no. 4 (Winter 1963): 9–18; and my "Rules and Exceptions in Ethics and Aesthetics," *Philosophy and Phenomenological Research* 27, no. 2 (December 1966): 267–73.

17. Kierkegaard, *Fear and Trembling*, p. 72.

18. Ibid., p. 27.

19. Ibid., p. 86.

20. Martin Buber, "The Suspension of Ethics," in *Four Existentialist Theologians*, ed. Will Herberg (Garden City, N.Y.: Doubleday, Anchor Books, 1958), p. 227.

21. Kierkegaard, *Fear and Trembling*, p. 41.

22. Geoffrey Clive, "The Teleological Suspension of the Ethical in Nineteenth Century Literature," *The Journal of Religion* 34, no. 2 (April 1954): 75–87.

23. Henrik Ibsen, *Brand* (Garden City, N.Y.: Doubleday, Anchor Books, 1960), p. 87.

24. Ibid., p. 99.

25. Ibid., pp. 135–36.

26. Ibid., p. 98.

27. Clive. "Teleological Suspension of the Ethical," p. 80.

CHAPTER IV

1. Sören Kierkegaard, *Concluding Unscientific Postscript* (Princeton, N.J.: Princeton University Press, 1941), p. 189.

2. Sören Kierkegaard, *The Sickness Unto Death* (Garden City, N.Y.: Doubleday, 1954), p. 218.

3. Sören Kierkegaard, *Stages on Life's Way* (New York: Shocken Books, 1967), pp. 415–16.

4. Kierkegaard, *Concluding Unscientific Postscript*, p. 543.

5. Ibid., p. 513.

6. Ludwig Feuerbach, *The Essence of Christianity* (New York: Harper and Brothers, 1957), p. 135.

7. Ibid., p. 213.

8. Frank Allen Patterson, ed., *The Student's Milton*, rev. ed. (New York: Appleton-Century-Crofts, 1933), p. 18.

9. Feuerbach, p. xxxvii.

10. Robert Herbert, "Two of Kierkegaard's Uses of 'Paradox'," *The Philosophical Review* 70, no. 1 (January 1961) : 53.

11. Kierkegaard, *Fear and Trembling*, pp. 46–47.

12. Herbert, "Kierkegaard's Uses of 'Paradox'," p. 54.

13. Kierkegaard, *Philosophical Fragments*, p. 71.

14. See my article "Kierkegaard's Uses of 'Paradox'—Yet Once More," *Journal of Existentialism* 7, no. 27 (Spring 1967) : 319–28. See also, in the same issue, the article by Alastair McKinnon, "Kierkegaard: 'Paradox' and Irrationalism," pp. 401–16.

15. Kierkegaard, *Concluding Unscientific Postscript*, p. xv.

16. Ibid., p. 178.

17. Ibid., p. 180.

18. Ibid., p. 105.

19. Höffding, *A History of Modern Philosophy*, 2:288.

20. Ibsen, *Brand*, p. 145.

21. Dru, *The Journals of Kierkegaard*, p. 142.

22. Ibid., p. 166.

CHAPTER V

1. Kierkegaard, *Philosophical Fragments*, p. 5.

2. This interpretation of Plato's epistemology is fairly standard. The reader will find it set forth in various works. One competent source is W. T. Jones, *A History of Western Philosophy*, vol. 2, *The Classical Mind*, 2nd ed. (New York: Harcourt Brace and World, 1969), especially chap. 4, "Plato: the Theory of Forms," pp. 108–46.

3. Kierkegaard, *Philosophical Fragments*, p. 6.

4. Ibid., p. 9.

5. Ibid., pp. 9–10.

6. Ibid., p. 10.

7. Ibid.

8. Marjorie Grene, *Introduction to Existentialism* (Chicago: University of Chicago Press, 1959), p. 33.

9. Kierkegaard, *Philosophical Fragments*, p. 12.

10. Ibid., p. 13.

11. Ibid., p. 92.

12. Kierkegaard, *Concluding Unscientific Postscript*, p. 18.

13. Henry E. Allison, "Christianity and Nonsense," in Josiah Thompson, ed., *Kierkegaard: a Collection of Critical Essays* (Garden City, N.Y.: Doubleday, 1972), p. 291. The essay first appeared in the *Review of Metaphysics* 20 (March 1967).

14. G. W. F. Hegel, *The Phenomenology of Mind*, trans. by J. B. Baillie (New York: Macmillan, 1961), p. 85.

15. Ibid., p. 130.

16. William J. Kilgore, *An Introductory Logic* (New York: Holt, Rinehart and Winston, 1968), p. 235.

17. Kierkegaard, *Concluding Unscientific Postscript*, pp. 45–46. See also Allison, "Christianity and Nonsense," p. 290.

18. Allison, "Christianity and Nonsense," p. 290.

19. Kierkegaard, *Concluding Unscientific Postscript*, p. 107.

20. Paul Edwards, "Kierkegaard and the 'Truth' of Christianity," *Philosophy* 46 (April 1971): 101.

21. Kierkegaard, *Concluding Unscientific Postscript*, p. 155.

22. Edwards, "Kierkegaard and the 'Truth' of Christianity," p. 99.

23. Ibid.

24. Emil Brunner, *Truth as Encounter*, new ed. (Philadelphia: Westminster Press, 1964), p. 21.

CHAPTER VI

1. Dru, *Journals of Kierkegaard*, p. 95.

2. Paul Roubiczek, *Existentialism: For and Against* (Cambridge: Cambridge University Press, 1964), p. 55.

3. Translated by Lowrie, *Kierkegaard*, 2 vols. (London: Oxford University Press, 1938), 1:xii.

4. Erich Kinkler, "Martin Heidegger," in *Christianity and the Existentialists*, ed. Carl Michalson (New York: Charles Scribner's Sons, 1956), p. 115.

5. For two good discussions of Jaspers's impact for theology see David E. Roberts, *Existentialism and Religious Belief* (New York: Oxford University Press, 1959), p. 227 ff. and Wild, *The Challenge of Existentialism*, p. 151 ff.

6. Karl Jaspers, "Epilogue 1955" to his *Philosophy* (Chicago: University of Chicago Press, 1969), 1:9.

7. Daniel Jenkins, "Karl Barth," *A Handbook of Christian Theologians*, ed. Dean G. Peerman and Martin E. Marty (Cleveland: World, 1965), p. 420. See also David L. Mueller, *Makers of the Modern Theological Mind: Karl Barth* (Waco, Tx.: Word Books, 1972).

8. Lowrie, *Kierkegaard*, 1:vi.

9. Thomas F. Torrance, "Karl Barth," *Union Seminary Quarterly Review*, 12 (November 1956) : 23 ff.

10. J. Heywood Thomas, "The Christology of Sören Kierkegaard and Karl Barth," *Hibbert Journal* 53 (April 1955) : 288.

11. Karl Barth, "A Thank-You and a Bow: Kierkegaard's Reveille," *Canadian Journal of Theology*, 13 (January 1965) : 7. See also Karl Barth, "Kierkegaard and the Theologians," *Canadian Journal of Theology* 13 (January 1967) : 64–65.

12. Dagobert D. Runes, ed., *Pictorial History of Philosophy* (New York: Philosophical Library, 1959), p. 340.

13. Dagobert D. Runes, ed., *German Existentialism* (New York: Philosophical Library, 1965).

14. Michael E. Zimmerman, "Heidegger, Ethics, and National Socialism," *The Southwestern Journal of Philosophy* 5 (Spring 1974) : 98.

15. Details of Heidegger's life are to be found in many recent books. One good source is Joseph J. Kockelmans, *Martin Heidegger: A First Introduction to His Philosophy* (Pittsburgh: Duquesne University Press, 1965).

16. John Macquarrie, *An Existentialist Theology: A Comparison of Heidegger and Bultmann* (New York: Harper & Row, 1965) ; Morris Ashcraft, *Makers of the Modern Theological Mind: Rudolf Bultmann* (Waco, Tx.: Word Books, 1972).

17. Macquarrie, *An Existentialist Theology*, pp. 69–71.

18. Ibid., p. 91.

19. For a discussion of this point, see Herbert C. Wolf, *Kierkegaard and Bultmann: The Quest of the Historical Jesus* (Minneapolis: Augsburg, 1965).

20. Sören Kierkegaard, *Training in Christianity* (Princeton, N.J.: Princeton University Press, 1944), p. 28. S.K. was struggling with the question raised by Lessing, the 18th-century rationalist. The problem of the supposed gap between bestowed fact and religious faith is often called "Lessing's Ditch."

21. Rudolf Bultmann, "The Case for Demythologizing: A Reply," trans. R. H. Fuller, *Kerygma and Myth*, vol. 2, ed. H. W. Bartsch (London: S.P.C.K., 1962), p. 192.

22. For a clear discussion of these and other related issues, see Thomas C. Oden, *Radical Obedience: the Ethics of Rudolf Bultmann* (Philadelphia: Westminster Press, 1964), especially p. 25 ff. and p. 111.

23. Translated and quoted by Oden in *Radical Obedience*, p. 111.

24. Paul Tillich, *Perspectives on 19th and 20th Century Protestant Theology*, ed. Carl R. Braaten (New York: Harper & Row, 1967), p. 162.

25. Ibid., p. 163.

26. Paul Tillich, "Autobiographical Reflections," in *The Theology of Paul Tillich*, ed. Charles W. Kegley and Robert W. Bretall (New York: Macmillan, 1964), p. 11.

27. Ibid., p. 14.

28. Paul Tillich, *Systematic Theology*, 3 vols. (Chicago: University of Chicago Press, 1951), 1:12.

29. Walter M. Horton, "Tillich's Role in Contemporary Theology," in Kegley and Bretall, *The Theology of Paul Tillich*, p. 30. For a more extensive description, see Kenneth Hamilton, *The System and the Gospel: a Critique of Paul Tillich* (New York: Macmillan, 1963), especially chapter 2.

30. See Malcolm L. Diamond, *Martin Buber: Jewish Existentialist* (New York: Harper & Row, 1968), especially p. 10 ff., p. 92 ff.

31. Gabriel Marcel, "Some Reflections on Existentialism," *Philosophy Today*, 8 (Winter 1964): 248–57.

32. See Emil Brunner, *The Divine Imperative: a Study in Christian Ethics* (Philadelphia: Westminster Press, 1947). The index shows twenty-two (!) references to S.K. See also Emil Brunner, *Revelation and Reason: The Christian Doctrine of Faith and Knowledge* (Philadelphia: Westminster Press, 1946), especially chap. 25; and N. H. Söe, "The Personal Ethics of Emil Brunner," in *The Theology of Emil Brunner*, ed. Charles W. Kegley and Robert W. Bretall (New York: Macmillan, 1962), pp. 247–61.

33. See Richard Kroner, "The Historical Roots of Niebuhr's Thought," in *Reinhold Niebuhr: His Religious, Social, and Political Thought*, ed. Charles W. Kegley and Robert W. Bretall (New York: Macmillan, 1956), especially p. 182 ff.

CONCLUSION

1. Perhaps it is not too late to call attention to an excellent recent essay on Kierkegaard's ethics by John D. Glenn, Jr., "Kierkegaard's Ethical Philosophy," *The Southwestern Journal of Philosophy* 5 (Spring 1974): 121–28.

BIBLIOGRAPHICAL ESSAY

1. Thomas J. McCormack, review of *Sören Kierkegaard als Philosoph* by Harald Höffding, *The Monist* 7 (October 1896), p. 137.

2. Lilian M. Swenson, in her preface for David F. Swenson's *Kierkegaardian Philosophy in the Faith of a Scholar* (Philadelphia: Westminster Press, 1949), p. 8.

3. Vol. 25, no. 4, July 1916, pp. 567–86.

4. Rev. ed. (Minneapolis: Augsburg, 1948).

5. William K. Stewart, *Hibbert Journal* 27 (January 1929): 228.

6. Arthur Liebert, "Contemporary European Philosophy," *Philosophical Review* 40 (January 1931): 45.

7. *American Scandinavian Review* 17 (October 1929): 591–99.

8. See the review by T. M. Greene, *Journal of Philosophy* 35 (1938): 663–65.

ANOTHER "CONCLUDING UNSCIENTIFIC POSTSCRIPT"

1. Kierkegaard, *The Sickness Unto Death,* p. 260, n.